WINDMILLS and WATERWHEELS EXPLAINED

Machines that Fed the Nation

STAN YORKE

COUNTRYSIDE BO
NEWBURY BERKSHIF

D1381394

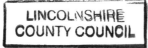
First published 2006
© Stan Yorke 2006

COUNTRYSIDE BOOKS
3 Catherine Road
Newbury, Berkshire

To view our complete range of books,
please visit us at
www.countrysidebooks.co.uk

ISBN 1 84674 011 8
EAN 9781 84674 011 4

Photographs and line
illustrations by the author

Produced through MRM Associates Ltd., Reading
Typeset by CJWT Solutions, Newton-le-Willows
Printed by Borcombe Printers plc, Romsey

CONTENTS

Acknowledgements

uring the research for this book I have been delighted by the enthusiastic help and advice I have received from the staff and helpers at numerous mills. Possibly because many are run by part-time 'amateurs', they are only too happy to talk about their mill and its restoration and running. Whatever the reason, I thank you all for your patience and interest.

My particular thanks go to Martin Hanson of Heckington Windmill for reading through the draft and making comments and corrections. Lastly, and by no means least, I must thank my wife, Margaret, for her endless patience whilst I disappeared for hours working on the book.

Woodbridge Tidemill.

Introduction

It is amazing to discover that there are well over 400 waterwheels and windmills open to the public in England and Wales, many of them still working. It is as though (secretly placed around the countryside) there are portals to a time, not just a century or two ago, but back a thousand years or more.

It was whilst researching for my book *The Industrial Revolution Explained* that I came across the superb work of modern-day restorers in bringing back to life these ancient machines. Like many early working machines these have blended completely into the countryside and, I suppose, because they feature in every turn of our history they seem to be natural features – hardly man-made at all.

But what of their history and how do they work? In keeping with the rest of the 'England's Living History' series of books, I have set out to explain the background and development of both waterwheels and windmills without recourse to overly technical terms. Indeed, part of their charm is their deceptively simple mechanisms which hide a great deal of knowledge and ingenuity.

One of the few industrial sites still active – Cheddleton Flint Mill in Staffordshire.

This link to the past is not all that it seems, though. Look at a windmill or watermill today and for all the world it could have been unchanged for centuries. This, however, is not quite true! These are working machines, they were virtually our only industrial power source from the Roman occupation until the arrival of steam in the 1700s and, like all industrial processes, they were updated and rebuilt as new ideas arrived. What we see today are mostly mills from the late 1700s and early 1800s that have been lovingly restored, often from complete dereliction. Unlike castles and houses which still stand, the link with early times lives on in the sites and occasionally in the materials.

In many cases, there has been a mill on the site right back to medieval times, particularly watermills.

The book is split into three sections. Section I provides an overview of the mills from the earliest times right up to their demise in the 19th century. In Section II we get our hands dirty and look in detail at the processes and workings of the mill machinery. In order to simplify what at first can seem a bit chaotic I have discussed the turning of grain into flour in chapter 5 and in chapter 6 I have shown the mechanics of the drive systems and how the power from the sails or wheels gets to the stones. Section III brings us up to date with the work of restoration and

Derbyshire mill stones resting after many years of work, at Daniels Mill near Bridgnorth in Shropshire.

the latest uses of wind and water power. It then gives some thought to finding mills to visit, plus giving a glossary of terms.

You will note a very heavy bias towards flour milling because, quite simply, this activity is by far the most common in the restored mills we can see today. Where I have come across working sites that illustrate some of the other uses that windmills or waterwheels were put to, I have included a picture and notes.

The book is generously illustrated with photos and drawings and will, hopefully, arouse your interest and add to the enjoyment of visiting.

Stan Yorke

Post Mill

Smock Mill

Tower Mill

Undershot Wheel

Breastshot Wheel

Overshot Wheel

The basic types of windmills and waterwheels.

Classic post mill with bricked-in base timbers at the Avoncroft Museum of Historic Buildings. The post with the wheel at the end is used to turn the mill into the wind.

SECTION I

THE
STORY
OF MILLING

CHAPTER 1

A Brief History

Like so many early features in history, our knowledge is based on the distilled comments and interpretations of many different chroniclers. This leads to a variety of opinion that can seem difficult to resolve and indeed this confusion is very true of our earliest machine – the waterwheel.

What seems generally agreed is that man used the flow of water in a river or stream to power simple mechanisms at least as long ago as 200 BC. There are three basic devices that are known from early Roman times: the horizontal waterwheel, often called a Norse wheel; the Noria; and the undershot vertical waterwheel. Some claim the Norse wheel comes from earlier centuries in Greece but others suggest that the evidence for this is very weak. Indeed, some suggest that it might well have come last of the three. What we do know is that all three machines were widely used and survived in various forms into the 19th century, with a few making it into the 20th century.

The horizontal wheel consisted of a vertical shaft around the bottom of which were fixed radial boards or paddles. The water flow was directed at these paddles so that it caused them, and the shaft, to rotate. The rotating shaft was used to directly turn a grindstone to make flour.

The very earliest versions adjusted the gap between the grinding stones (a feature, as we shall see, that was very important) by a system of wedges set into the shaft, but very soon this was replaced by the 'tenter beam' or 'bridge tree', as shown in Fig 1.1. This beam carries the

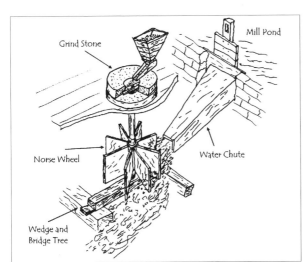

Grind Stone

Mill Pond

Norse Wheel

Water Chute

Wedge and Bridge Tree

FIG 1.1: *Possible arrangement of an early horizontal wheel flour mill. The arrangement of the stones and the way the grain was fed had been established by the Romans and remains virtually unchanged to this day. This type of wheel became known popularly as a Norse wheel.*

bottom bearing of the vertical shaft including the paddles and the top 'runner' stone. By adjusting one end of this beam the top stone can be raised or lowered, thus altering the gap between the stones, a process known as tentering. These wheels were relatively simple to construct and could also turn a modest-sized grindstone using very little water flow. Its simplicity made this type of wheel common in small rural communities and some were still in use up to the last century in Scotland and Ireland.

The vertical wheel is the type we think of as the traditional water wheel. The paddles are set on a much larger diameter than the Norse wheel and the shaft that holds them is horizontal, carried in two bearings. The Noria was a variation of the vertical wheel used to lift water and was a self-contained machine that did not drive anything else. It consisted of a wheel which carried around one side a series of pots or buckets. The bottom and the lowest pots were in the flow of a river, which turned the wheel.

The pots filled with water at the same time and were carried, rather like a big wheel at a fairground, up to the top where they would empty their contents into a trough, which carried the water away. Used for irrigation and water supplies to towns, they were built to surprisingly large diameter – certainly up to 50 ft (15 m) and possibly larger.

Roman engineers developed a variation on this theme, where they devised an undershot wheel to turn a separate 'chain of pots'. This used water containers, sometimes earthenware pots, sometimes wooden boxes, which were strung together to form a continuous loop. The bottom of the loop dipped into the river and the top tipped the water-filled pots into a wooden channel, thus directing the water as required. They were normally driven at the top and thus required gears and shafts from the waterwheel, so not only could they be used to raise water from a river but the same 'chain of pots' could be driven at the top and used to lift water up from a shaft or mine.

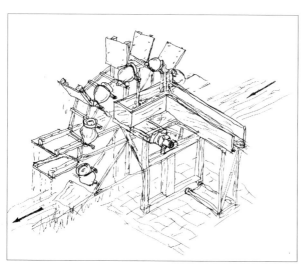

FIG 1.2: *This figure shows the principle of the Noria. The pots are held out from the wheel in order to pass over the receiving trough. There are quite a few drawings of what historians believe the Noria may have looked like but, alas, many are not mechanically feasible!*

The main use of the traditional vertical wheel was always to turn grindstones to make flour, though the rotating horizontal shaft of these waterwheels could also power hammers and certainly it was used to crush stone from the very beginning. The horizontal shaft, however, is no use for grinding flour and here the breakthrough almost certainly came from the Romans – gears.

The first gears were used simply to take the power from the rotating horizontal shaft and turn it through 90° to drive a vertical rotating shaft. It didn't take too long before the engineers realised that by making the gear wheels of different sizes, it was possible to alter the speed of the vertical shaft. The earliest mills seem to have been made with the gears giving a slight reduction in speed to the vertical shaft and we must assume that these needed a fast-flowing river or stream to create a fast-turning wheel. We must also remember that these early mills still used a version of the old hand-turned style of grindstone, shaped rather like an hourglass, called a quern. (See Fig 5.2) It took a while before the flat stones, that we think of today, were developed. We must also remember that at first these

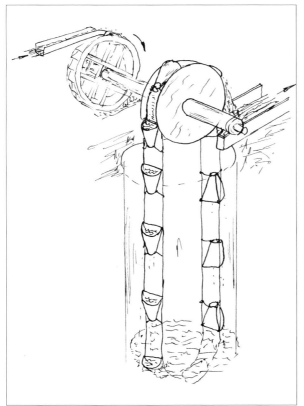

FIG 1.3: *Chain of Pots. Our knowledge of these devices is fairly limited. They were most commonly driven by men or horses. Getting water for the wheel was usually a problem – mines and streams are rare companions! There must have also been a fair waste of water when the pots turned over as the trough catching the water has to have a gap to allow the pots to descend again.*

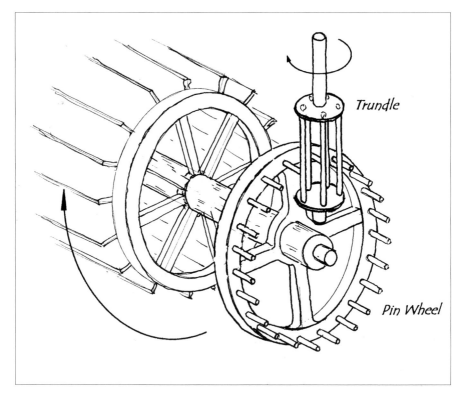

Trundle

Pin Wheel

FIG 1.4: *Early Roman gearing using pins (pin wheel) and a trundle (which was rather like a simple bird cage) where the pins mesh with vertical bars of the cage. Relics of this very old gear system can still be found.*

early waterwheels were relatively rare.

Up to around AD 250 the Roman Empire still used its abundant supply of slaves and cheap labour as the normal power source. As the Empire began to ebb this labour source started to shrink and by AD 350–400 the Romans were putting serious effort into constructing waterwheels to replace their slaves. Roman writers also describe breastshot and overshot wheels though these seem to have been only rarely used at this stage. Indeed the breastshot wheel had to wait

for a better understanding of waterwheels before it really blossomed. In Britain there is evidence of Roman use of waterwheels not just for grain but for driving hammers to crush ore.

We must remind ourselves that all this was going on some 2,000 years ago! Whilst the Romans used iron for small items, the majority of these structures would have been made entirely from wood, as indeed they would be for the next 1,500 years.

The Romans eventually left our shores

around AD 400 and the next 700 years became known as the Dark Ages. Originally 'Dark' because there seemed to be so little evidence of what life was like during this period, slowly, research is filling in more detail. However, despite several invasions and many regional battles, life went on. The monasteries tended to make what we might call the scientific advances – they dominated iron-making and improved agriculture – but everywhere the humble waterwheel continued to grind flour and crush stone and ore. All large monasteries and estates would have had their own waterwheel-driven mills and indeed the notorious system, where tied tenants were forced to use the local manorial lord's mill (soke rights), was well established in these times. Many defensive castles had mills built within the walls in order to survive periods of siege. They sometimes used water from the moat, though that seems somewhat unwise when you are being attacked.

By the time of the Domesday Book in 1089, some 5,000 mills were recorded at over 3,000 different sites. It is possible that at this time the Norse wheel still outnumbered the vertical wheel and both still usually drove just one pair of grinding stones.

FIG 1.5: *An unusual estate mill on the Chatsworth estate. Built in the late 1700s in a style to match the rest of the estate, it worked into the 20th century but was destroyed when three trees collapsed onto the building in a storm!*

Around 1100, another use for the waterwheel was found; one that was to become second only to grinding flour, and that was for fulling woollen cloth. This process involved washing and pummeling the new woven cloth in water, with various other ingredients like fuller's earth.

The process helped to shrink the cloth and at the same time it bound the fibres together and fluffed up or 'fulled' the cloth. Originally done by hand, it adapted easily to waterwheel-driven hammers.

Windmills

During the 12th century, windmills had spread from the Middle East through the Mediterranean countries and then slowly up through northern Europe. The original mills were fixed stone buildings carrying four sails, shaped rather like children's windmills. These had developed in areas that had a dominant wind direction and there was no provision to move the sails.

The cup-like shape of the sails would collect energy over a fairly wide angle so the mill would turn in nearly all wind conditions. However, northern Europe has far more fickle winds that can blow from virtually any direction. Somehow the sails would have to be turned – the first solution was simply to turn the whole building!

The post mill, as it is called, is a small self-contained mill set upon a stout vertical post. It usually has a long pole fixed to the mill that extends towards the ground to enable the mill to be turned into the wind. These mills were used mainly for grinding flour but by having a hollow post the drive could be taken down and used to pump water. Windmills were the second choice in terms of skill and cost and were used where streams or

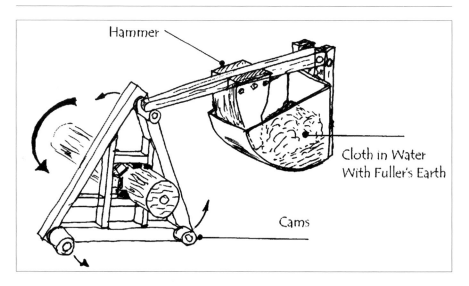

FIG 1.6: *A simple diagram showing a single hammer pounding the cloth. Fulling stocks soon developed to using a pair of hammers, one dropping as the other rose, thus adding an extra twist to the cloth as it was pounded.*

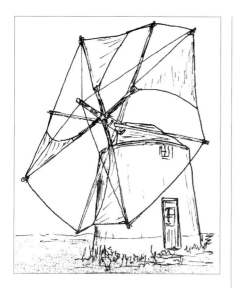

FIG 1.7: *Classic Mediterranean fixed windmill.*

wood rather than stone, but the principle is the same for both types. The smock mill was often used for drainage as its lighter weight meant it was easier to erect on the soft waterlogged ground of the fens. As soon as you have a stationary building you can do two things: make it bigger to increase the room for the milling, and make it higher to catch more wind and be able to use larger sails. Though the original reason for the development of larger windmills had been to obtain a rotating shaft that could be used to drive

rivers simply weren't to hand and to this day our eastern counties still have the greatest concentration of windmills in England.

The need to be able to pump water for irrigation and drainage steadily grew, particularly in countries like Holland. The Dutch engineers with almost no suitable rivers took the windmill to their hearts. Used to drive pumps, it was a prayer answered. Very soon they realised that it was only the sails that needed to be moved and if the downward drive shaft was placed in the centre of the mill then just the sails and the first gear wheel need be turned. Thus was born the tower mill. Early examples were straight-sided with a horizontal shaft carrying the sails but later versions inclined the sail shaft and had the more familiar tapered towers.

There was a variation known as a smock mill where the tower was built of

FIG 1.8: *Pitstone post mill in Buckinghamshire, thought to be one of the oldest windmills (around 1650) not to have been extensively altered.*

water pumps, smock and tower mills flourished for flour making and here in England it became the main application.

By the 1300s the vertical waterwheel dominated and one authority has suggested that by 1400 there were over 6,000 waterwheels and over 3,000 windmills at work in England. This was, however, the period of the Black Death and the plague's subsequent eruptions and there is no doubt that by the 1500s

FIG 1.9: *This extensively restored post mill, in Gt Gransden, Cambridgeshire, dates from the 17th century and shows just how precarious they looked. It is also rare in that the sails turned clockwise.*

FIG 1.10: *The moving gear on the post mill shown on page 9. The long lever raises the steps off the grass whilst the winch pulls the mill around using the rope and the posts set in the ground every few yards around the track. It's slow and hard!*

FIG 1.11: *An early (1760) tower mill near Ashton in Somerset. The overhanging part of the cap houses the turning gear operated by a chain loop which hangs down to the ground. This is a rare example of a mill built with straight sides and with the sail shaft parallel to the ground instead of being tilted.*

many mills had become unused and derelict.

The first attempts to increase the output of a mill involved making the waterwheel drive a second pair of stones via a lay shaft and gearing. This second pair of stones usually turned faster than the originals and were thus often smaller in size.

During the 15th to 18th centuries the making of iron steadily improved and became fairly widespread. The key requirement in the production of cheap iron was the use of bellows to drive a steady blast of air through the charcoal fire used in the furnaces, and the waterwheel became the usual method of driving these bellows. The iron foundries and forges also adopted the waterwheel to drive their hammers, making the simple waterwheel the vital tool in the expansion of the iron industry and a key ingredient of the Industrial Revolution.

In this period both waterwheels and

FIG 1.12: *Chailey smock mill. Sited in the centre of Sussex, this mill had been moved twice before coming to rest here in 1864. Now devoid of its internal machinery it houses a small museum of rural life. Thankfully its external condition is immaculate.*

windmills made use of the advances in ironwork to improve their own performance until, around the late 1700s, we reached the stage that is still embodied in a few of our oldest restored mills today. One major change was to introduce the great spur wheel, which enabled two, three or even four identical sets of grindstones to be driven. Originally wood, like all the gears, these massive wheels soon became cast in iron.

Most of our remaining mills, though, are from the early 1800s and make extensive use of cast iron. We must also

remember that these machines were the 'factories' of their day, incorporating any improvement or modification that made the work easier or more profitable.

And what of the miller himself? He was paid in flour – typically he was allowed a one-sixteenth share of the flour milled but as it was he himself who judged just how much this was, inevitably he was often suspected of taking more. He also was thought to under-declare how much he had milled, thus reducing his payments to the lord of the manor as well. This bad reputation was given much credence by

FIG 1.13: *As the wheels became larger they provided more energy and a second vertical drive via a lay shaft could be added. Still using the pin wheel and trundle gears, this second shaft turns faster than the original and was often fitted with a smaller set of stones.*

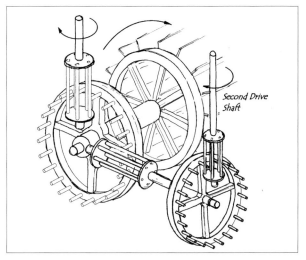

FIG 1.14: *One of the many fine buildings to have been re-erected in the Weald and Downlands Open Air Museum in Sussex. Originally built in the 17th century in Lurgashall, the mill has been restored to working order and produces flour for sale.*

FIG 1.15: *A fine example of a mill site that started as a small medieval mill serving the nearby Abbey and grew as the local town expanded. This is Abbey Mill in Tewkesbury, now converted to housing. The River Avon was in flood when the picture was taken and one of the two waterwheels can just be seen half submerged.*

Chaucer who in the prologue to his Canterbury Tales says:

His was a master's hand at stealing grain,
He felt it with his thumb and thus he knew
Its quality and took three times his due -
A thumb of Gold, by God, to gauge an oat.

He was, nevertheless, a hardworking and strong man and one the people needed. Before the 18th century he or his assistant would collect the grain on a horse-drawn cart, carry the sacks up the mill ladders and repeat this tough routine in reverse after the milling, to deliver the flour.

I hope that these brief notes will help relate these wonderful machines to our earliest times long before canals, trains or vehicles transformed the way we live.

FIG 1.16: *Brindley's Mill in Leek, Staffs, now dwarfed by more recent, and ugly, factory buildings. Started in the early 1700s, much altered over time but now beautifully restored inside.*

CHAPTER 2

Science and Iron Arrive
1700–1800

❧✦❧

By the early 1700s mathematicians had started to analyse the workings of both the waterwheel and the windmill. One such academic was Antoine Parent who, in 1704, presented his ideas on the optimum design criteria for waterwheels. All thoughts were concentrated on the effects of water impacting upon the blades of the wheel. Even for an overshot waterwheel it was assumed that the impact of the water was all that mattered. Parent's ideas, soon extended by Henri Pitot, became completely entrenched in the scientific literature of the time and were still being printed in the *Encyclopaedia Britannica* into the 1800s.

Doubts started to appear during the mid 1700s and climaxed in the first thorough practical tests carried out by John Smeaton, here in England. Smeaton's results showed that Parent's figures were in error and that the weight of the water descending – particularly in the overshot wheel – was very significant. Similar work followed here, in France

FIG 2.1: *A breastshot wheel where the water pours onto the wheel roughly in line with the axle. This wheel dates from around 1850 and replaced an earlier wheel inside the mill. On later wheels the stonework follows the curve of the wheel and prevents too much of the water spilling out too early as the wheel revolves. One can just make out where the control shaft for lifting the sluice enters the mill so the miller can control the speed from inside. This is Alderholt Mill in Hampshire.*

FIG 2.2: *One of two overshot wheels that serve the Dunster Mill in Somerset. These are fed by a narrow leat that follows the lane down to the mill. Note the wheels are still all wood – spokes, shaft and buckets.*

and in Italy and by the 1780s the various factors affecting efficiency and power output were understood for the first time.

Following the realisation of the importance of the weight of the water rather than its impact, around 1780 many undershot wheels were converted to breastshot wheels, giving greater efficiency. This involved raising the water level, a problem solved by either taking the leat from higher up the valley or else by forming a mill pond. So we now have

some impact energy but also we have the weight of the water sitting in the buckets and forcing these downwards. 'Buckets' isn't quite the right word – the boards were simply altered to hold water in place. These breastshot wheels became the most common form of wheel, with many preserved today.

The theoretical work carried out by Smeaton and others had also shown that for maximum efficiency breastshot and particularly overshot wheels should turn slowly, with gearing used to obtain the necessary speeds within the mill.

Later improvements 'boxed in' the breastshot wheel so that little water could escape the buckets until they were virtually at the bottom. This made use of the weight of every last drop of water and improved the efficiency figures to around 35%.

The remaining type of waterwheel was the overshot wheel, where the water is introduced right at the top of the circle, thus making maximum use of its weight. These were normally built where it was easy to obtain a water feed much higher than the mill – steep, small valleys being the favourite situation. One feature of an overshot wheel is that it turns the opposite way to undershot and breastshot wheels. This had the problem that when the water reached the bottom of the wheel it was going in the wrong direction

– it required space in order to turn and rejoin the natural flow of the stream. An even bigger problem was that during times of flood, the high stream level at the bottom of the wheel meant that the buckets actually hit the water – but the stream was going the opposite way to the buckets and thus acted as a brake.

To overcome this the pitchback wheel was developed where the water was still taken to the top of the wheel but turned back to enter the wheel the opposite way. Occasionally a breastshot wheel has been converted to an overshot wheel and the use of this reversing trick means the mill equipment still turns the same way as it did with the breastshot wheel.

The amount of energy that could be taken from the water depended on how far the water falls whilst contained within the waterwheel. Thus an overshot wheel could be made narrower than the same

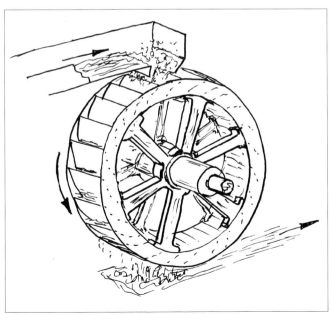

FIG 2.3: *A pitchback wheel where the water is taken to the top of the wheel but reversed in direction. The wheel now turns in the same direction a breastshot wheel would have done.*

output breastshot wheel. This in turn meant it used less water so, if the stream was limited in the quantity of water it could supply but could be brought to the wheel at a high level, then the overshot wheel was the best solution.

The overshot wheel could attain efficiencies of 60% to 70% and was now designed to have a peripheral speed of around 3 ft per second. In a 30 ft (9 m) diameter wheel that means a rotation speed of just two revolutions per minute.

As iron became more widely available during the 16th, 17th and 18th centuries, waterwheels grew in size and power. Early in the 1800s engineers (possibly Strutt or Hewes) realised that the process of taking all the energy from the paddles or buckets down to the central shaft and then speeding up the rotation by using gears could be simplified. By fitting a large cast-iron ring gear around the wheel itself and then driving a pinion gear from this, two benefits were obtained. Firstly, the naturally high gear ratio gave a high-speed shaft rotation from the relatively slow wheel. For the same power, a higher speed shaft meant less torque and thus

FIG 2.4: *Suspension wheel with a slightly smaller ring gear. This rebuilt wheel is in the Hereford Water Works museum. The gear ring can be seen bolted to the spokes. Often this gear ring is cast as part of the rim of the wheel.*

FIG 2.5: *The end of a spring sail with the mechanism locked open. The shutters, the little cranks and the shaft that moves the cranks can be seen on this close up from Greens Mill in Nottingham.*

lighter shafts and bearings and this saved money. The second benefit was that the power from the buckets was no longer taken down the spokes to the central shaft and there was thus almost no torque in this shaft at all. The only job the spokes now performed was to hold the weight of the wheel (known as a suspension wheel) and keep it in shape – they simply experience tension. The spokes and the centre shaft could be made lighter and again cheaper. This technique of taking the power from a bolt-on iron peripheral gear ring was also applied to existing wooden waterwheels, the lighter loading on the spokes and shafts simply extending the life of these already substantial timber structures.

These improvements to waterwheels were applied to all the various industries, including milling, but they didn't really alter the operation, they simply provided greater efficiency.

Windmills also benefited from a steady series of improvements but these were directed at making life easier and safer. The first was the move away from loose cloth 'common' sails to sails using shutters, rather like a venetian blind, known as 'spring' sails. The shutters were held closed by a spring so that a strong gust of wind would be able to push the shutters open, allowing the wind to pass through the sail rather than increasing its speed. The miller could stop the sails turning, adjust the spring tension and then release the brake to allow the sails to turn again.

Later on, this system was improved by having a small diameter shaft (called the striking rod) which ran through the centre of the main windshaft. At the sail end, the new striking rod was attached to a set of bell cranks which, in turn, controlled the shutter position. By moving the inside end of this shaft to and

FIG 2.6: *A diagrammatic cross section of the patent sail mechanism. The miller would set the chain as he wanted and then hang a weight at the lowest point of the chain or rope loop. A gust of wind would push the shutters which would raise the weight but when the gust passed the weight would pull the shutters back to their original setting.*

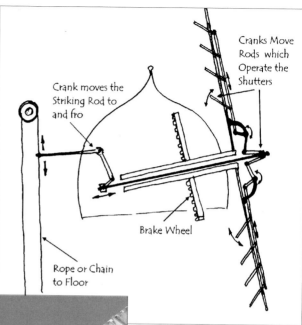

Cranks Move Rods which Operate the Shutters

Crank moves the Striking Rod to and fro

Brake Wheel

Rope or Chain to Floor

FIG 2.7: *The spider where the striking rod emerges from the windshaft. Using cranks, the movement is turned through 90° to operate the shutters. This is Shipley mill in Sussex, the last working smock mill left in the county. Note the sails with a smaller set of shutters to one side of the stocks. The stocks are the main beams that carry the sails.*

FIG 2.8: *If you thought that the previous picture looked complicated, then have thoughts for those who restored Heckington Mill in Lincolnshire. This is the largest eight-sailed mill left in Europe.*

fro, the angle of the shutters could be set whilst the sails were turning. Usually this mechanism was adjusted by a chain or rope loop which hung down to the reefing gallery or ground level.

For the first time the miller had some real control over the power source and speed of his mill. This idea had been patented and these sails became known simply as 'patent' sails. They had one slight drawback in that for the same size they produced slightly less power than the common sail – even when closed they still 'leaked' air. Many mills were built with one pair of common sails and one pair of 'patent' sails to give the miller a wide range of options.

A further automatic feature was added. Rather than just alter the shutters using the rope loop, if a weight was hung at the bottom of the loop then a strong gust of wind would push the shutters further open and this movement being sent via the cranks and the striking rod, would raise the weight. Once the gust subsided the weight would pull the rope back to its original position thus resetting the shutters to their original position.

The other onerous task – turning the sails to face the wind – was also improved. Early tower mills had mechanical systems for turning the cap. The most common was a cast ring gear set around the top of the tower into which a gear pinion would engage. This pinion was turned by a series of gears which were rotated by a large pulley set outside the cap. This pulley was turned by a rope or chain which hung down to the floor or the gallery where it could be operated by the miller.

To automate this job, a small wind sail was set at right angles to the main sails and the drive from this taken into the cap, where it drove gearing which, in turn, rotated the cap. The fantail, as it is known, will only turn when it is facing across the wind but once it is in the line of the wind it will cease turning. This is exactly the point at which the main mill sails are facing directly into the wind. As the wind changes direction, the fantail

FIG 2.9: *An early external mechanism to turn the sails. Originally a rope would have turned the wheel which then turned the wooden worm drive. This engaged in the ring gear mounted around the top of the tower.*

FIG 2.10: *A pre-fantail mill showing the external pulley and rope. The gears etc are housed inside the cap. Note the 'upturned boat' cap on the Bursledon Mill in Hampshire.*

will start to rotate and, in turn, move the cap around until the main sails once again face the wind. The gearing is set such that the fantail has to turn many times to move the cap just a few degrees so that it doesn't constantly move in response to every little gust. It also needs this high gearing in order to develop sufficient power to move the cap and the main sails, which often weigh in excess of three tons. Even post mills had fantails fitted to their turning posts, producing a very strange looking arrangement.

One problem with the fantail was that if the wind had been blowing, say, from the east, then died down and possibly a day later picked up again but from the west, the fantail would not turn. It was after all still in the line of the wind but the main sails were now 180° wrong, known as being 'tail-winded'. The wind pressure was now trying to turn the sails the wrong way and worse still was trying to blow the sails away from the tower.

FIG 2.11: *The fantail on the Heage Mill in Derbyshire. The drive shaft that takes the drive into the cap can just be seen behind the fan blades.*

FIG 2.12: *A large post mill built in 1821 and moved to this spot, high on the South Downs in Sussex, in 1852. This is 'Jill', restored after years of neglect. 'Jack', a tower mill, now privately owned, is to the right. The fantail drives a pair of wheels which trundle around on a stone track set in the ground, taking the tailpole with it.*

FIG 2.13: *The guide wheels that keep the cap in place, this time in the Maud Foster Mill in Boston (see page 41). The cap slides around on a well oiled track which bears the weight. In many windmills a set of small wheels are used to bear the weight and make turning a little easier.*

FIG 2.14: *Don't panic! This is looking up into the cap of Heage Mill. The striking rod mechanism is centre left. The rest is the drive from the fantail – the gear ring can just be seen running around the edge of the tower. All fantail systems include the facility to disengage the sails and turn the cap manually.*

FIG 2.15: *A cast iron sailshaft showing the 'canister' which held the two sail stocks. This shaft has provision for the striking rod to pass through it in order to operate the patent shutters.*

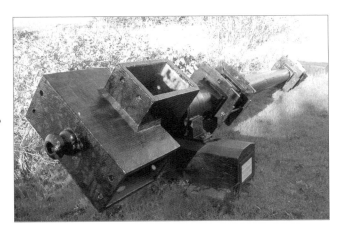

This thankfully rare situation, which wrecked mills in the past, was handled by being able to disengage the fantail drive and manually turn the cap around.

As with waterwheels, iron was used to replace wood, particularly in shafts and gears. The main windshaft benefited most, with its difficult task of holding the sail stocks whilst having another small rod passing through its centre.

In waterwheels, shafts with much simpler brackets to hold the spokes became common. We must also remember that the wooden waterwheel wore out much sooner than the internal machinery and thus was rebuilt many times during the working life of a mill. Each rebuild would use the current ideas and materials giving rise to the oft-seen 'modern' all-iron wheel driving beautiful old wooden machinery inside the mill.

One last development was still to come, the governor. This was a mechanism which used centrifugal force to provide a 'signal' which indicated the speed of a shaft. In flour milling, both watermills and windmills, this was used to adjust the gap between the stones dependent on the speed they are turning, by using a series of

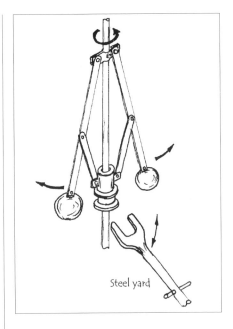

Steel yard

FIG 2.16: *Diagrammatic view of a governor. Everything except the fork turns with the shaft. As the speed rises the two weights move outwards pulling the sliding bearing upwards, thus moving the steel yard as well.*

FIG 2.17: *A common arrangement where the governor is driven by a belt – which often indicates that the governor had been added later. This is inside Shipley Mill in Sussex, a smock mill once owned by Hilaire Belloc. Note the wooden construction of the outside walls.*

FIG 2.18: *This governor, in the Maud Foster Mill, operates like a pair of scissors producing a downward movement which is fed to all three tenter beams via the three steel yards.*

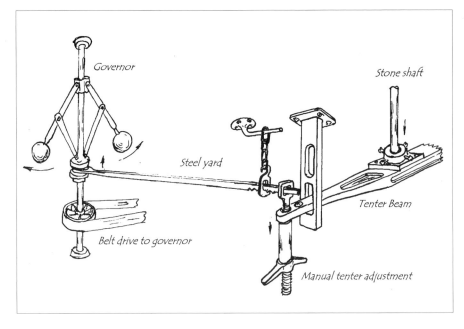

FIG 2.19: *Diagram showing how the governor alters the tentering. Imagine the speed has increased, the weights swing further out, lifting the steel yard. The steel yard pivots so that the far right-hand end now drops, which in turn lowers the tenter beam thus reducing the gap between the stones.*

FIG 2.20: *A good example of the use of iron. This is the brake wheel and wallower gear in the Wilton windmill in Wiltshire. Note the main drive shaft setting off on its journey down the mill, is also iron.*

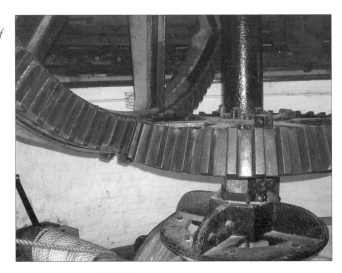

FIG 2.21: *A rare novelty, a hollow post mill water pump from the 1850s. Originally from near Pevensey, it has been erected in the Weald and Downland museum in Sussex. It drives a pair of cast-iron lift pumps, just visible through the fence, which raised water. The size is deceptive as the entire pump including the sails is only around 12 ft (4m) high.*

FIG 2.22: *This view, looking up from the balcony, shows the use of cast iron to make the 'sail cross' that holds the sails in the Maud Foster Mill. This windmill is one of only eleven that survive from the original 500 that were built in Lincolnshire.*

levers from the governor to the tentering beam. These were called steel yards, though the exact arrangement varied from one mill to the next. The miller still controlled how much of this adjustment the governor made and naturally still retained overall control of the process. This was particularly useful for windmills where the sail speed can vary continuously, causing the miller to be forever adjusting the tentering.

In water-driven mills that had a mechanical process like grinding stone or driving machines there was no tentering, but it was desirable to keep the drive system at a steady speed regardless of the load and the governor on these systems was adapted to control the flow of water into the leat and thus affect the wheel speed. This idea was later copied by steam engine designers to control the speed of their engines.

FIG 2.23: *An unusual situation: a Suffolk village which still has a windmill and a water mill, both fully restored and working! This is Pakenham Windmill which dates from 1830.*

FIG 2.24: *Like many watermills that were built where a lane crossed over a stream Pakenham Mill, from the 1780s, has a large mill pond (set behind the mill to the left) from which the water flows through the mill and under the road. It is easy to drive straight past such buildings as there is little except the style to indicate that here is a working flour mill. Note the use of black pitch to weatherproof the brickwork on both buildings.*

CHAPTER 3

The Zenith of Local Milling
1800–1850

The period from around 1780 to 1830 saw the full blossoming of the Industrial Revolution. Everywhere, iron was making industry easier, larger and more profitable. Despite the invention of the steam engine a hundred years earlier, its development had been slow. Mighty steam-driven, beam pumping engines were now common and by 1800 there were probably around 1,000 such engines in use, but still around 18,000 waterwheels.

Smaller steam engines were being developed but for much of the first half

FIG 3.1: *Cogglesford Mill, Sleaford. The present building dates from the early 1800s and represents the pinnacle of local milling. Like so many such mills it is a mixture of materials from much earlier mills that were built on the same site.*

of the 19th century their cost simply left the waterwheel supreme. It wasn't just the initial cost either: watermills and windmills were constructed and maintained by long established craftsmen – the millwrights – and the materials and techniques were well known and pretty basic. The steam engine needed water, coal or coke, regular maintenance and it took time and skill to light it up at the start of the day and to close it down at the end. Water and wind were free and the machinery could be started or stopped in minutes. All these factors enabled the water and wind machines to survive alongside the new-fangled steam engines rather than being replaced by them.

Most of the surviving structures we can visit today date from this period, either built as new or as substantial rebuilds. The confidence of the engineers, aided by iron, grew until we had some very impressive machines built well into the late 1800s.

FIG 3.2: *A unique representative from Warwickshire, not from the age of follies but much earlier, in 1732. Updated in the 1860s, this is Chesterton Windmill.*

FIG 3.3: *For many years the only mill left on the river Thames, Mapledurham Mill is a delight. Full of wooden machinery, it seems timeless. In fact, it was extensively restored quite recently but retains a real old world feel.*

FIG 3.4: *Lincolnshire has many beautifully restored working mills. This is the Maud Foster Mill in Boston. It's the tallest commercially working mill in the country and unusually has five sails. The high balcony is used mainly to adjust the patent sails and apply the brake. Note the onion-shaped cap, the proper name for this shape being ogee. It is most common in Lincolnshire. This is still the original cap – a rare claim for working restored mills.*

FIG 3.5: *This time in Lincoln itself, the Ellis Mill, built in 1798, stands over the town, the last of nine built on the Lincoln ridge. Many tower mills were painted with a black pitch to achieve total dryness – essential where flour is being handled and bagged.*

One aspect of these water- and wind-driven machines that can seem odd to us today is the way they were often moved or rebuilt. To understand this better we have to shed the romantic image of bygone days and Constable's paintings – these mills were the industry of their day. Their sole purpose was to do a job of work and do it cheaper than any other method. That they seem so visually appealing is simply the way that time has mellowed the noise, dust and stark newness that they would have had 200 years ago – from leading technology to quaint relics in one leap!

Scientific progress did, however, continue. In the case of windmills the development of the wind engine spread around the world. Using aerodynamically more efficient sails – usually metal – they took over the job of pumping water, particularly from wells. Needing virtually no attention and working day and night if there was some wind, they became the supreme pump for water supplies away from rivers. One source suggests that some six million of these machines were made in America alone.

FIG 3.6: *Alderholt Mill, built on a very old site which dates back to at least the 1300s. It's driven by an external breastshot wheel, which replaced the original internal wheel, fed by a tributary of the Hampshire Avon.*

FIG 3.7: *Two windmills from the Midlands. Greens Mill, in Nottingham, was built in 1807 on an earlier mill site. It is fitted with one pair of cloth sails (common) and one pair of spring sails. A brief sketch of the struggle to restore this mill is given in Chapter 8 though most mills we see today went through similar pain.*

FIG 3.8: *Further still from the traditional eastern counties, Heage Windmill in Derbyshire was built in 1797 and is the only six-sail mill in the county. Built just three storeys high, a reefing gallery isn't needed.*

FIG 3.9: *Heckington Mill is the largest eight-sail mill to survive in Europe. Originally it had five sails but these were destroyed in a storm. In 1892 the present eight-sail assembly was moved from another mill in Boston.*

FIG 3.10: *Like most windmills still working today, Wilton Mill in Wiltshire was built in the 1780-1830 period. Featuring a pair of patent sails and a pair of common sails, it continued working into the 1920s. Its arrival was due to rather unusual circumstances – the nearby valley had five waterwheel-driven mills but in 1808 the Kennet and Avon Canal was driven down the same narrow valley destroying all five. This single windmill was built to replace them – an indication that perhaps there was not that much work.*

FIG 3.11: *White Mill, Shapwich in Dorset. This is possibly unique – a mill that was rebuilt in 1776 on a much earlier site. Boarded up for many years, the National Trust decided to preserve rather than restore it, giving us a wonderful picture of an old atmospheric mill. Superb guides tell the amazing story of its rescue and the work that was needed to stabilise the building.*

On the waterwheel front two developments occurred, one a delightful culmination of study of the waterwheel and its efficiency, the other the first real progress in developing the 2,000-year-old idea of the Norse wheel.

Though breastshot and overshot wheels could now produce efficiencies of over 60% there were many sites that because of their geography could only use the old undershot wheel. The undershot wheel was also still the best if a high speed of rotation was needed and a suitable river existed. The study of waterwheels had led to the notion that, for maximum efficiency, water should enter the wheel with no impact and leave the wheel with no velocity. Impact wasted some of the force and water leaving the wheel still moving had obviously not given up all its energy.

A French engineer, Jean Victor Poncelet, worked on this problem and designed an undershot wheel which

FIG 3.12: *The wind engine in Crux Easton, Hampshire. This superb example, built by John Wallis Titt of Warminster, is a Simplex self regulating machine used to pump water from a well and later also to grind corn. Erected in 1892, it has 48 sails set in a 20 ft diameter wheel which can be adjusted – the centre ring controls the angle. It also has a fantail to keep it facing into the wind. It represents the advances made late in the 1800s. Relatively cheap to mass produce, this type of wind engine lasted well into the 20th century.*

reached efficiencies of over 60%, more than twice those of conventional undershot wheels. The way the water was fed into the wheel was vital to its working and his use of a sloped, sliding hatch rather than a simple up-and-down sluice gate enabled the water to enter the curved blades and to rise up the blade. The entry speed, that is the water's kinetic energy, was thus exchanged for weight, or potential energy. As the wheel turned, the weight of the water having done its job, the water virtually dropped from the blades into the tail race, i.e. with no forward velocity left.

Another French engineer, Alphonse Sagebien, designed a variation on the low breastshot wheel which worked on a very slow water speed and again produced remarkably high efficiency, certainly in excess of 70%. Despite small quantities being made in England from the 1820s,

both these developments were largely ignored outside France!

This was possibly rather a shame because Poncelet had hit on an idea that worked in a different way to conventional wheels. The energy came from the fact that the water moved within the blades, first rising to fill the space between them and then dropping as it left. By turning this wheel to the horizontal plane – like the old Norse wheel – we have the basics of the water turbine. Poncelet himself even suggested this, adding the idea that the water might enter around the periphery and exit at the centre thus eliminating the reversal that occurs in the vertical version.

Yet another Frenchman, Benoit Fourneyron, took up these ideas and developed the first successful horizontal water turbines, reaching efficiencies of over 80%. Usually the water was

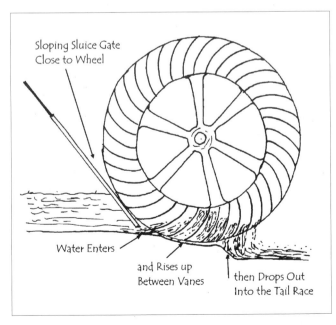

Sloping Sluice Gate Close to Wheel

Water Enters

and Rises up Between Vanes

then Drops Out Into the Tail Race

FIG 3.13: *The basic principle of the Poncelet wheel. Rather than hitting the paddle the water now rises up between the curved blades and then drops out into the tail race. There has been very little impact and the water leaving the blades has almost no forward velocity left.*

introduced at the centre, flowed through all the blades to the periphery where it was collected and fed away. Note one simple but very important difference – all blades are contributing energy all the time, not just those carrying water as in the conventional waterwheel. The turbine had other useful features: it would still run if submerged in water and thus wasn't stopped if the river was in flood; and the shaft was vertical and rotated at a much higher speed thus simplifying gearing. It also has one big disadvantage, from our point of view – it's completely encased and thus totally invisible. Several turbine-driven mills still exist though little of the turbines can be seen.

FIG 3.14: *A rare sight, an early turbine on display at the Cauldwell Mill in Derbyshire. The water entered via the large pipe on the right, passed through a control gate and then hit the saucer-shaped blades. Its energy spent, the water left via the top and bottom openings. The centre shaft, now rotating, rose upwards into the mill. Cauldwell still generates its own electricity using a turbine.*

FIG 3.15: *Sarehole Mill in suburban Birmingham – sole working survivor of many mills that served our second city.*

FIG 3.16: *Cauldwell Mill in Derbyshire, home to many later developments such as roller mills and turbines.*

CHAPTER 4

From Front Line Industry to Lonely Backwater

T he period from the 1850s to the 1930s is remarkably short when one considers the life span of the waterwheel and the windmill, yet in those few years nearly all passed into history. The process was at times quite complex with pressure from many different areas rendering the earlier machines uneconomic.

The milling of flour succumbed to a purely profit-motivated change.

Millwrights in Austria had developed a roller mill using porcelain rollers, sometimes used to refine coarse 'middling' flour. The rollers, however, wore down rapidly, a problem solved in Hungary by using iron rollers. The rollers could be set to any gap and this allowed them to be set to simply crack the grain – rather like a nut. Sieving followed this stage, removing the bran. A second pair of rollers set closer removed the

FIG 4.1: *An early French-made roller mill with porcelain rollers, on show in the Cauldwell Mill.*

FIG 4.2: *Another basic roller mill with cast-iron rollers made in the 1880s in Retford. Used for animal feed, this is in the Maud Foster Mill in Boston.*

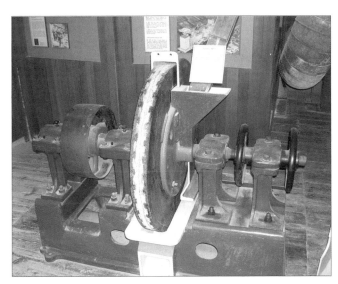

FIG 4.3: An unusual vertical carborundum mill on display in Cauldwell Mill, dating from around 1910. The left-hand stone is turned whilst the right-hand stone is adjusted to control the gap. Used to break down bran to be added to animal feed.

FIG 4.4: A riverside 'modern' roller mill in Tewkesbury, the Borough Flour Mills, an extension of the older Healings Mill. It is still active though the grain is no longer brought up the river Severn by barges from Sharpness harbour. The last two redundant barges can be seen tied up in front of the mill.

FIG 4.5: *The classic waterwheel mill converted to housing. The wheel pit is still intact, converted to a simple weir. This is one of many mill conversions on the river Thames; only the shape and style of the structure gives its original purpose away.*

wheatgerm and lastly a further pair of rollers crushed the endosperm to produce an almost pure white flour. It was very efficient and lent itself to producing refined flour very easily.

At the same time, in America, mechanisation allowed vast fields of grain to be grown, way beyond the amount needed by America herself. Yet again, as if by some ordered chance, ships were now being built that would make short work of bringing the cheap American grain to Europe. The American grain was hard and well suited to the new roller mills. Some mills converted from revolving stones to roller machines but the fact that the cheaper grain was coming by ship started the building of vast roller mills where the ships could unload directly. Even inland, where a river provided good transportation from a major port, roller mills appeared. A glance at the map of England will show just how many of our cities are on rivers and near ports, and so the mass demand for flour was now met by these massive roller mills.

FIG 4.6: *A hotel complex, this time built around a redundant windmill. This is within the Milton Keynes area – who says all modern developments lack character?*

FIG 4.7: *One of several Thames conversions though in this case the owners have restored much of the mill machinery. The waterwheel is still in place but when run created so much vibration that the owners decided that it all looked just as nice stationary!*

FIG 4.8: *Braunston Windmill. This sort of conversion is quite a common sight, where the mill tower has been adapted for living with virtually all machinery removed, though not all are as handsome or in such a lovely position as Braunston.*

FIG 4.9: *Another house conversion, this time a waterwheel-driven mill. The stream still flows under the road and house giving away its original use.*

FIG 4.10: *A very unusual adaptation – the mill is still there, restored following a disastrous fire and still working to produce flour occasionally. It now forms a feature of the hotel restaurant, though one has to wonder how many of the hotel guests realise the history just next door. Longbridge Mill is in Hampshire.*

Away from these areas local milling by waterwheel and windmill continued and indeed many such small mills carried on in production into the 1940s and 1950s but it was a struggle to make a profit.

The flour mills that lost out in this dramatic change could rarely adapt to any other use. Most new industry demanded larger amounts of power and the steam engine had by now developed into a reliable machine. Today these mills are either completely gone or have been converted to housing or hotels though many smaller towns and villages still have a 'Mill Lane' or a 'Mill House'.

The fate of the other industrial, non-flour producing, waterwheel sites followed a similar trend, only this time it was straightforward progress. Whatever industry they had been associated with, that industry was expanding, needing bigger premises, larger power sources and the flexibility of the steam engine. By the start of the 20th century diesel engines were finishing off any remaining pockets of the older power sources.

Throughout this whole period, another aspect of life in England was also slowly changing. Transport – first the canals, then the railways and lastly the vastly improved roads – removed yet another advantage of the local mill. Being local to

FIG 4.11: *This is one of a pair of modern wind generators near Dereham in Cambridgeshire – not really the obvious place to find them! Though graceful in engineering terms, they can be seen for miles and are not everyone's choice of scenery.*

the town you once served no longer mattered – just the price.

Though representing just a small fraction of the waterwheels and windmills of the 1850 peak, a few specialist industrial uses lingered on into the 1950s just as a few flour mills had done.

Today we see the new electricity-generating wind farms spread out over high ground, though understandably some are none too popular with the locals. Tidal generators have been talked of for many years, with plans to build barriers across major estuaries such as the River Severn, but I wonder how many realise that there were once many tidal mills. Indeed, there are three such mills preserved, one still producing flour, but their power is minute compared to the needs of the national grid! Perhaps the eventual demise of fossil fuels will drive man to reapply these early principles of using nature's free energy and continue a line of progress so rudely interrupted by the steam engine all those years ago.

FIG 4.12: *A delightful working site – Abbeydale Industrial Hamlet in Sheffield. Nestling below a vast mill pond, this water-powered scythe works survived as a specialist site into the 20th century. Now much restored it gives a fascinating insight into 18th and 19th century working conditions.*

FIG 4.13: *The massive Coxes Mill on the River Wey navigation just 16 miles from the centre of London and now converted to apartments. As with many 'modern' mills around London the grain was delivered by barge right up to 1960.*

SECTION II

INSIDE

THE

MILL

CHAPTER 5

Milling

Waterwheels and windmills were primarily used to produce flour, the key ingredient in our staple diet. When man first realised the food value of powdered grass seeds is open to debate but there is no doubt that it was well established by 2000 BC. This early flour would have been mixed with water to produce a dough which was then flattened out and baked, producing what has been described as a 'badly made pie crust'. The Egyptians are credited with the discovery of fermentation which allows the dough to rise before baking, producing a more aerated bread. Originally the natural yeast in the dough was used but later yeast was added just as it is today. Leavening, as this stage is called, is mentioned in the Bible around 1250 BC.

Some time prior to 2000 BC, Neolithic man had brought wheat, barley and oats

FIG 5.1: *Scooped out stone or saddle quern on display in the Cauldwell Mill.*

to Britain and the Saxons added rye to these grains around 500 AD. Wheat is the grain used today for flour but prior to 1800 rye was used extensively for bread flour, as it still is in continental Europe. Barley is used mainly in brewing and oats

FIG 5.2: *Diagram of a rotary hand quern with the top stone cut away to show the centre.*

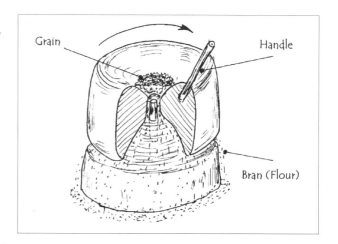

in oatmeal and porridge but both are also used for animal feed.

The earliest method was to grind the grain in a scooped out stone using a smaller hand-held stone to apply the pressure and movement. Some of these old stones have been found and are on display in the restored mill sites. In Egypt the grain was often pounded using a mortar and pestle. Both methods lasted into the 20th century in some remote parts of the world.

By Roman times the idea of using two shaped stones, one of which revolved on top of the other, had been developed. The shape of these 'querns' differed over the centuries but all followed the same basic principle. Grain was admitted via a hole into the gap between the stones and rotation ground the seed down to produce a simple flour. This rotation was at first provided by hand or animals but it was a natural step to use the power of water, and later, wind to do the turning.

The Romans even had animal-driven machines to knead the dough and bakers

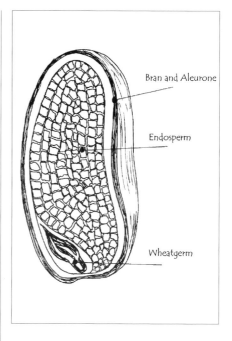

FIG 5.3: *Cross section of a grain of wheat.*

FIG 5.4: *Classic 'modern' dressing of the working face of the stones. This example is from Bursledon Mill, in Hampshire.*

were organised and controlled by the state. After the Romans left these shores bread making seems to have reverted to a purely domestic activity until the 13th century. Nevertheless, we retained the knowledge of waterwheel-driven mills using flat rotating stones.

Until around 1850 the grain was ground into flour without any part being removed; this is wholemeal flour. By sifting the wholemeal flour through sieves of various grades, it is possible to remove proportions of the bran and wheatgerm to give a whiter flour. Wheatmeal flour has around 20% of these parts removed and Hovis has 28% removed and then some of the wheatgerm put back. White bread has all the bran and wheatgerm removed but this leaves the flour so low in vitamins that it is artificially fortified to replace some goodness! The demand for white flour was primarily just a fashion and though it lasted for some 150 years, we are now able to get a wide range of breads based on wholemeal flours. One

of the reasons many modern flours lack the bran and wheatgerm is to enhance their keeping properties. The oils in the wheatgerm reduce the storage time of true stoneground flour to just a few weeks.

From quite early on it was realised that if the stones had grooves cut in them (called dressing), the grain was broken down much faster. The grooves were cut at an angle to the edge of the stone and when one stone was turned over and laid onto the other, these grooves lay at opposite angles. The action of the grooves passing over each other was rather like a pair of scissors – the grain was repeatedly cut rather than crushed and was naturally driven towards the outer edges. In between these deep grooves finer lines were cut, called stitching, which crushed the cut grain seed to produce the flour.

The upper (runner) stone was also very slightly dished so that the outer edge had a smaller gap than the centre. It was in this outer area, where the speed

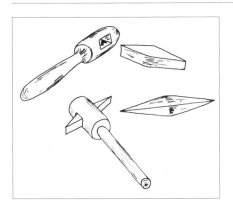

FIG 5.5: *Basic dressing tools with bill and chisels.*

FIG 5.6: *A selection of tools on display at Bunbury Mill in Cheshire.*

difference between the stones was greatest, that the majority of the work was done.

Dressing the very hard stone was a skilled job, sometimes done by the miller but often by a travelling stone dresser. The job involved removing the hopper, shoe and horse (the frame that supports these items) and then the tun or vat that encased the pair of stones. A simple form of crane was used to lift off the runner stone, turn it and lay it down for dressing. No easy task as the runner stone could weigh up to 1¼ tons!

The special chisels used lost small particles of metal during dressing, and naturally small pieces of stone also flew off. Before the days of health and safety these particles would embed themselves in the unprotected arms of the stone dresser. Indeed, his skill and experience would be judged by the extent of these marks when he 'showed his metal'. A pair of French burr stones could easily take a full week to re-cut, plus each chisel lasted for only one full groove. The stone dresser would arrive with dozens of freshly sharpened chisels and when all were blunt they would be taken back to the village smithy or a local forge to be resharpened.

The stones themselves were made from very hard rock. For coarser flour and animal feeds Derbyshire gritstone was used, with the entire stone cut from a single piece. This material whilst hard still deposited a fine grey stone dust into the flour as it wore down. For best flour the stones were made from the extremely hard French burr stone – a form of water quartz found near Paris. This occurs in pieces too small (or too expensive) to make a whole stone, so they were shaped and set in plaster of Paris with iron bands, called tyres, around the outside.

FIG 5.7: *Top side of a French burr runner stone showing the four balance pockets – here three are covered with one left open and empty. This is an example of a factory made stone – the oval plates give the maker's details and the date.*

FIG 5.8: *Stone lift and balancing crane used to lift, turn and balance the top stones. These were often positioned between a pair of stones so that both could be served or sometimes the crane could be moved and erected as needed.*

a little wider than for wholemeal. This leaves the bran larger and thus easier to sieve out later.

Though this is not at first obvious, the stones relied on the grain to keep them apart whilst they were turning – the top revolving stone was free to rock and without any grain would touch the stationary bed stone at the edges causing rapid overheating and damage. The working gap was between a fiftieth and a hundredth of an inch (0.25mm–0.5mm) so it doesn't take much movement to cause trouble. Though this gap was mechanically set there was nothing to stop the runner stone from being raised up on the grains, nothing that is, except its weight. This is why the runner stone was so heavy and it was common for the thickness of the runner to be built up from local stone like flint until the weight was right.

Like so many early machines the flour mill had various simple but clever devices to control the grinding process.

The main job was to maintain the flow of the grain seeds into the stones at a steady rate. This process relied simply on gravity; the grain was stored in hoppers one floor above the stones and was

These can last for hundreds of years in a small mill which only grinds occasionally though they have to be redressed every six months or so. The runner stone also had to be balanced using lead weights so that it didn't shake from side to side as it spun.

The grain remained between the stones for around three to four revolutions before it left the outer edge as meal. A typical pair of stones turning around 125 to 150 times per minute would produce 56 lbs (25 kg) of flour (strictly speaking, meal) in around 20 minutes. When producing white flour the stones were set

FIG 5.9: *Side view of a burr stone, with the tyres removed, which has been bulked up using local stones.*

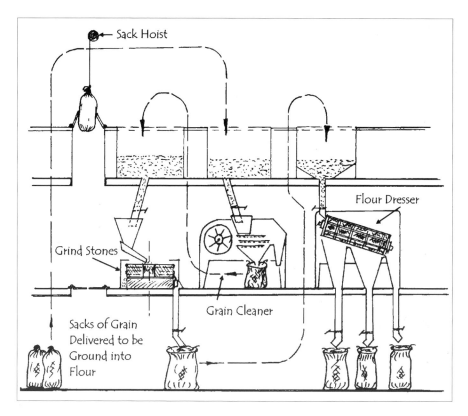

FIG 5.10: *The overall journey taken by the grain in a typical watermill. The layout in a windmill has similar machinery set out over more floors but these floors are of course much smaller in area. Though many mills have grain cleaners and flour grading machines on show they are very rarely in operation.*

directed down a wooden 'pipe' or chute (called a spout) and into a small local hopper above the stones. The end of this spout was set so that as the level of the grain rose in the local hopper it reached the end of the pipe and thus blocked it enough to stop any further grain from descending. As this grain level fell during grinding, more grain dropped again until the end of the pipe was covered once more.

The local hopper fed the grain down a funnel into a 'shoe' or 'slipper' and by altering how close the shoe was to the hopper funnel the rate of flow could be controlled. The angle of the shoe was set by a length of cord (the 'crook' string) which passed over the hopper supports and down to the floor below where the miller could control the flow rate. An alternative method used an adjustable slider, again controlled from below.

The reason for dropping down a floor was that the flour left the stones and fell through another wooden spout to the lower floor and into the waiting sacks. It was here that the miller could feel the temperature and fineness of the flour which, in turn, told him if the grinding was correct. Incidentally, the flour had to be swept into the down pipe and this was done by a small brush or metal blade which was attached to the iron bands around the runner stone.

Before returning to this lower floor two more clever features need explaining. The grain might not flow along the shoe or slipper on its own so a shaking action was added, just the same action as you or I would use to get grain to move steadily down the gentle slope before falling into the centre of the stones. This was obtained by gently pulling the shoe sideways using a piece of string attached to a length of springy wood. The shoe now rested against a shaft called a 'damsel' which was part of the drive system to the top stone. This is a three- or four-sided section which imparted the shaking motion as the shaft turned. The faster the stones turned the more vigorously the damsel shook the shoe – simple!

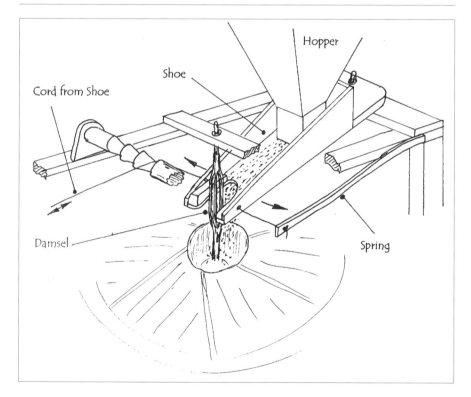

FIG 5.11: *Diagrammatic view of the grain feed to the grinding stones. This shows the basic principles but there are many variations both in the shapes and materials.*

FIG 5.12: *An unusual cast-iron horse frame holding the hopper and even a cast-iron shoe. This is in the Eling Tide mill in Hampshire.*

FIG 5.13: *The shoe complete with rubbing block being held against the damsel, at Stretton Mill in Cheshire.*

The last feature was the warning bell that let the miller know if the grain had run out. This was a most dangerous situation as the stones would touch each other causing very rapid heating and damage to the stones themselves. Again, the mechanism was simple, and yes, it uses string! A strap, often leather, was laid across the bottom of the local hopper attached by string to a small bell. The weight of the grain held the strap down and the bell was silent. Should the grain run out the strap would relax and rise allowing the bell to drop into a position in which it would ring, thus warning the miller on the floor below. The miller then had just a few minutes in which to stop the stones or feed more grain.

The other mechanism involved adjusting the gap between the stones but as this is closely tied into the main driving machinery it will be covered in the next chapter.

Up to the start of the 18th century the corn was grown, harvested and thrashed (or threshed, to be strictly accurate) with

FIG 5.14: *The warning bell mechanism to detect if the grain runs out. There are several variations but the principle is basically as shown.*

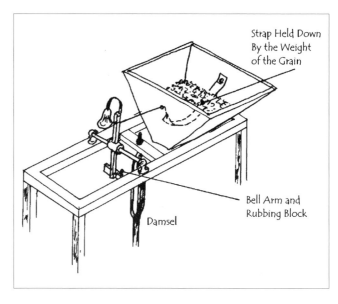

Strap Held Down By the Weight of the Grain

Bell Arm and Rubbing Block

Damsel

FIG 5.15: *Hand-operated grain cleaner. The rounded end (left) houses the fan. This example, in Bunbury Mill in Cheshire, gives great delight to youngsters who get to turn the fan as part of their tour of the mill.*

the resultant seeds being collected in sacks, in a process almost unchanged for centuries and basically unaided by machines. The seeds would be stored in barns – raised off the ground to keep the rats at bay – and kept dry until taken to be milled as and when the flour was needed. (Wholegrain flour can only be stored for a few weeks whereas the grain itself will keep for months.) Slowly, during the next hundred years or so, this process became mechanised, from horse-drawn seed drills and mechanical reapers through to waterwheel-driven and eventually steam-driven threshing machines.

In the mills themselves mechanically-driven sieves arrived to clean the grain of husks and debris before grinding. These machines, known as grain cleaners, used shaking sieves to separate the grain from the rubbish and a fan which blew air across the sieves to lift and move the chaff and other bits away.

Some grain cleaners used a rotary drum rather like the flour dressers.

A few old hand-turned grain-cleaning machines can still be seen though most were belt-driven from the auxiliary drive system. A variation of this was called a 'smutter', which used a vertical cylinder specifically designed to remove the spores of smut – a form of fungus which attacks wheat. Yet another cleaner was called a 'cockle cylinder' and was used to remove unwanted seeds from grass and wild flowers from the grain. Like many of the cleaning machines it was developed for white flour production.

One less obvious problem with the grain is how damp it is. Too much moisture will clog the stones and produce poor flour. Originally many mills had drying kilns where the grain would be dried before grinding. Some millers kept a small hand-mill or quern in which they would test grind a sample to check if the grain was dry enough and then to decide

FIG 5.16: 'Modern' hand-turned quern in the Town Mill, Lyme Regis. This is also used to allow children to try their hand at grinding – it's harder than you think!

FIG 5.17: *Rotary wire machine or flour grader. Most of these machines have lost their wire mesh sieves due to these simply rusting away.*

FIG 5.18: *Looking inside a wire machine – showing the rotary brushes that dragged the flour across the wire mesh.*

FIG 5.19: *A threshing machine from the early 1900s but representative of the steam engine-driven machines of the late 1800s. As well as separating the grain they also cleaned it of chaff and produced a grain ready for milling.*

on the stone gap and speed to use.

Yet more sieving machines, known as flour dressers, were employed to separate out the various grades of flour. Most common were the wire machines which consist of a drum covered in a fine wire mesh (originally cloth or silk). The drum sits at an angle and inside is a set of brushes which rotate, taking the flour (strictly called meal) around the inside of the drum, having been fed in at the top end from the grindstones. The finest flour would pass through the mesh leaving behind any bran or coarse material. In practice the mesh was usually graded into three sizes so that the finest flour passed through the first part of the mesh. The next section had a coarser mesh which collected the rougher flour (called 'middlings' or 'sharps') and the third mesh sieved out the bran used for animal feed. Anything which had not passed through the sieve would be expelled at the end of the drum as 'offal' or waste. This task could also be done by the shaking sieve-type of dresser. Again the size of the mesh controlled the quality of the resultant flour.

During the second half of the 19th century a new type of grain was produced, particularly in the USA and Canada, which was cheap and available in vast quantities. This was harder than our home-produced grain and did not grind well with conventional stones. As we saw earlier, this was to be the beginning of the end for traditional waterwheel and windmill milling.

CHAPTER 6

Turning the Stones

The majority of mills that can be seen today are flour mills so I will limit the description of the mechanics in this chapter to just producing flour. The differences between windmills and watermills are remarkably few and fairly obvious. In a windmill the power comes from the top of the structure whereas in a waterwheel-driven mill, this drive starts at the bottom. The other difference concerns the shape of the buildings. In a windmill it is possible to have many floors but each is limited in size, whereas watermills are often only two storeys high but each floor can spread over a considerable area.

The basic undershot waterwheel powered the earliest type of mill, with the water rushing past the bottom of the wheel, creating a turning motion which was carried along the main wheel shaft into the mill.

Here it turned the pit wheel which engaged with the wallower and thus set

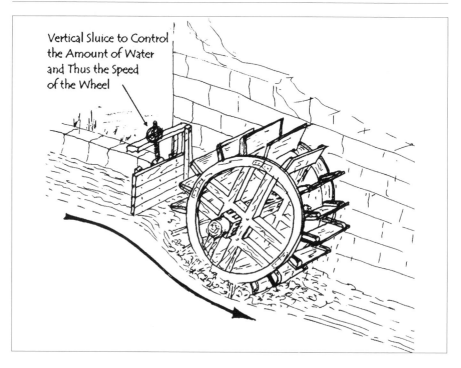

Vertical Sluice to Control the Amount of Water and Thus the Speed of the Wheel

FIG 6.1: *Cutaway drawing of the basic undershot waterwheel.*

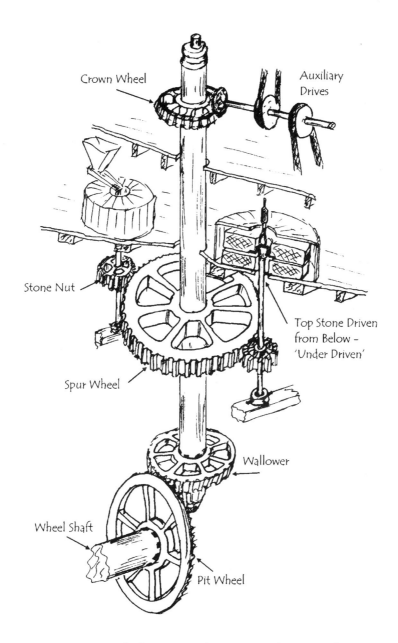

Crown Wheel

Auxiliary Drives

Stone Nut

Spur Wheel

Top Stone Driven from Below – 'Under Driven'

Wallower

Wheel Shaft

Pit Wheel

FIG 6.2: *The basic power drive system of a watermill.*

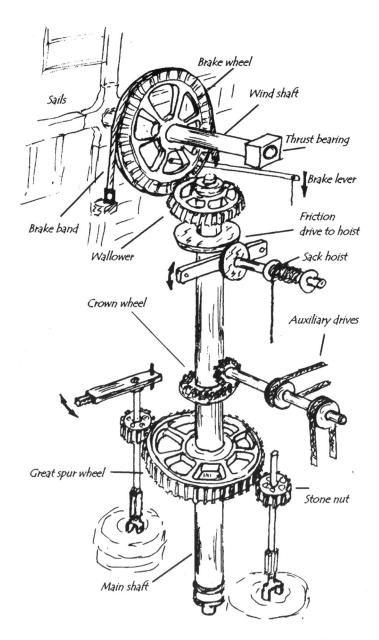

FIG 6.3: *The equivalent power system for a windmill.*

the vertical shaft rotating. Some of the gear wheel names make sense but many are old names which no longer mean anything to us today.

The speed of the wheel was controlled by a sluice gate which could be wound up or down, usually from within the mill building using gears or sometimes mechanical levers.

Let's now look in more detail at the mechanisms within the mill. Firstly the main wheel shaft – originally wood, usually oak, and carried in two wooden bearings. These would have to be kept well greased to prevent friction drying and eventually burning the wood. These bearings were later greatly improved by the use of iron gudgeons fitted into each end of the wooden shaft. Various shapes

were tried but all had two features in common – the short round pin that became the journal and the use of iron bands to reinforce the ends of the wooden shaft. The journal was usually in the order of 1½ to 3 inches (35 to 75mm) in diameter and between 3 and 6 inches (75 and 150mm) long. These turned in a bearing of wood (usually oak), brass or iron which in turn was set into a stone block or later bolted to the stonework of the mill.

The difficulty with the shaft is how to physically attach the wheel and the gear, plus the strength required to transmit the turning motion or torque. This last factor limited the size and power of waterwheels until the advent of cast-iron shafts. Two basic methods – clasp or mortised – were

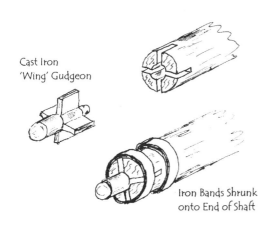

Cast Iron 'Wing' Gudgeon

Iron Bands Shrunk onto End of Shaft

FIG 6.4: *Gudgeon and prepared wooden shaft and bottom, the assembled shaft end reinforced by two iron bands. These are made just smaller than the shaft diameter, heated to make them expand, hammered onto the shaft and cooled down. This shrinks the iron to bind tight.*

FIG 6.5: *An old waterwheel shaft outside the City Mill in Winchester.*

FIG 6.6: *Examples of three construction methods – all wood (Dunster Mill), iron shaft and rim but still wooden spokes and paddles (Cheddleton Mill) and below, all iron (Alderholt Mill).*

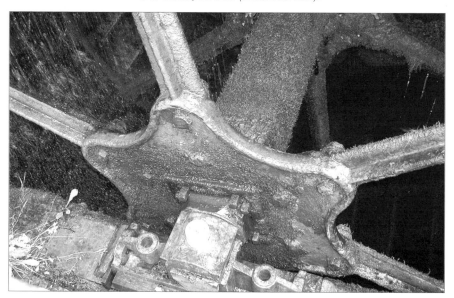

originally used to attach the arms or spokes. Mortising took the spokes into the shaft itself whilst in the clasp method the spokes enclosed the shaft – see Fig 6.1. The mortise method was generally preferred though requiring greater carpentry skills to make.

The arrival of larger iron castings produced iron rings that were fitted around the wooden shaft and provided individual brackets to which the arms could be fitted. Later cast-iron shafts became the standard complete with the brackets for the wheel arms.

The construction of the rims and paddles varied dependent on the choice of the millwright until the end of the 1700s

FIG 6.7: *Wooden teeth (or cogs). In this case the drive for the sack hoist in Stretton Mill.*

after which improved knowledge tended to make the type of wheel standard for each particular set of circumstances. Mortised joints aided by early iron nails and dowels (sometimes referred to as tree nails) were universally used in the construction until well into the 1800s.

The earliest gears were the peg and lantern type – again all wood. Later gears were the more conventional shape but with wooden teeth that could be replaced. By the 18th century cast-iron gears were in use. It was normal, however, for one of the two gear wheels to retain wooden teeth, which provided two important features – quietness and the ability to be easily renewed when they became worn. A good combination was for the larger wheel to be cast iron whilst the smaller one had wooden teeth made from apple or pear wood. The wood used for the gear teeth depended to some extent on the situation. If the gears can become wet then oak was preferred. For best performance hornbeam was the wood of choice but is now difficult to obtain in the right quality.

The vertical main shaft rose through the mill with power being taken off as required. These drives can be divided into three basic functions – driving the stones, driving auxiliary machines like cleaning and grading sieves and lastly, driving the sack hoist. In watermills with just two floors this led to seeming mechanical mayhem rather than the work of a sober miller.

Windmills follow almost exactly the same layout and, indeed, share similar problems. The main windshaft had to carry the weight of the sails and transmit the rotation to a vertical main shaft which descended through almost all the floors of the mill. The pit wheel now became the brakewheel but the other gears shared the same names as used in watermills.

FIG 6.8: *Bursledon Mill, near Southampton, showing an example of the boxed-in joint.*

FIG 6.9: *Mapledurham Mill, near Reading, with the wedges that hold the cast iron spoke ring onto the old wooden wheel shaft.*

FIG 6.10: *The miller at Bursledon Mill standing on the reefing gallery securing one of the sails prior to running the mill.*

The windshaft turned in two bearings and was usually set at approximately 15° from level to tilt the sails away from the building structure and to obtain greater efficiency in catching the wind. As with the waterwheel there were various ways to attach the sails to the shaft. Wooden shafts were sometimes mortised right through, and sometimes the sail stock was held onto the shaft end and then encased to produce a strong joint. As with the waterwheel, castings appeared in the early 1800s which fitted onto the shaft end and provided sockets through which the pine stocks passed.

Cast-iron shafts became common by the mid 1800s and incorporated all the necessary brackets. The outer bearing, nearest the sails, was sometimes just a half bearing relying on the weight of the sails to keep the shaft in place. The inside bearing was a thrust bearing able to hold the shaft and prevent any to or fro motion.

In both types of mill you will often see wedges holding the gears to their shafts. This allowed the gears to be removed but

FIG 6.11: *The brake wheel in the Wilton Mill showing one end of the iron brake band which could be tightened around the rim of the brake wheel. Even then it was not always possible to stop the sails in a really strong wind so the miller had to anticipate the winds very carefully.*

also to be centred. Indeed, in old mills where wood is extensively used you will see wedges used everywhere to tighten joints.

The windmill has a slightly different problem to the waterwheel when it comes to controlling the speed. With a waterwheel one simply controls the water flow – fairly basic and simple. The wind, however, won't respond to the miller's needs, so he has to be able to alter the sails – full for a gentle wind and trimmed down and small when the wind is high. The main sail used right up to the end of the 1700s was the 'common' sail in which the open frame was set to one side of the 'sail back' and carried a canvas sail held in position by ropes.

The sail frames were made with a twist (called weathering) rather like an aircraft propeller to give optimum aerodynamics. In these sails the miller physically altered the extent of the cloth sail – but to do this the sails had to be stationary. What he needed was a brake and that's exactly what windmills have. Normally placed around the rim of the brake wheel gear, it consisted of a set of wooden brake shoes, or sometimes an iron band, that could be tightened against the gear wheel rim to slow down and halt the sails. The miller then went outside and one by one adjusted the cloth on each sail. In tower and smock mills the sails were higher up and no longer reached down to ground level so a reefing gallery was built around

FIG 6.12: *The only remaining thatched cap left in England. This is the charming Stembridge windmill in Somerset, built in 1822 and now in the care of the National Trust.*

these mills which could be reached from inside and gave the miller access to the sails. As we saw in chapter 2, this control problem received great attention as the centuries went by and by the late 1700s the miller's life was considerably easier and safer.

The windshaft, the brakewheel and the bearings were carried on a massive frame which, in a post mill, formed part of the structure but which in tower or smock mills sat on a track (or curb) built around the top edge of the tower. The frame was sometimes on cast-iron blocks which were kept well greased and simply slid around, though often it was carried on small wheels. The shape of the track and the wheels was designed so that the frame was held in place and could only rotate – the side thrust on this system can be very high in strong winds.

The frame also carried the cap which encloses the top of the mill. These varied in shape and construction but all had the same job, to keep the windshaft and the various mechanisms dry and protected from the weather.

Having now obtained our vertical rotating main shaft in both wind and watermills, we can look at the three basic functions: driving the stones, driving auxiliary machines and lastly, driving the sack hoist.

Driving the Stones

The top stone (or runner) was carried on an iron hat-shaped saddle (rhynd or rynd) which in turn rested in a slot cast into a block (mace) that fitted onto the top of the stone spindle. The damsel also fitted onto this casting at right angles to the rhynd. The runner stone was free to rock on the rhynd and ought not to be turned until grain was present. The stone spindle passed down through the centre of the stationary bed stone via a bearing (neckbox). The space above this bearing was sometimes filled – often with plaster – to prevent the grain falling down through the bed stone. The bottom of the

FIG 6.13: *Some great spur wheels are greater than others! This monster, constructed with a combination of iron and wood, is in Brindley's Mill.*

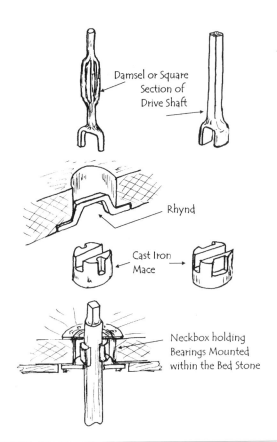

Damsel or Square Section of Drive Shaft

Rhynd

Cast Iron Mace

Neckbox holding Bearings Mounted within the Bed Stone

FIG 6.14: *Exploded view of the runner stone drive system. If the stones are 'overdriven' then the damsel is replaced by the heavier drive shaft (shown to the right) which, being square, still provides the shaking motion like the damsel. The weight of the top stone and the tentering is still carried by the lower shaft (stone spindle) even though the drive comes from above.*

stone spindle rested in a cup bearing carried on a beam called the bridge tree, which also had to bear the full weight of the runner stone. In an underdriven mill the stone spindle also carried the stone nut, a gear wheel which engaged with the great spur wheel fitted to our original vertical power shaft. The spur wheel had a greater diameter than the stone nut and this stepped up the stone spindle speed to the 100 to 150 revolutions per minute needed for grinding. It was usual to have two sets of stones driven from the spur wheel though mills with three sets are not uncommon. This simple description belittles two vital mechanisms, both of which display the ingenuity of the millwright. They also come in a bewildering variety which can be confusing.

Before looking at these I must mention that in some mills the runner stone was held and adjusted as described but the drive came from above – called overdriven, more common in windmills. The damsel was replaced by a stronger shaft which rose above the stones and had the stone nut near its top. This shaft had a square or irregular section which replaced the damsel. It still engaged with

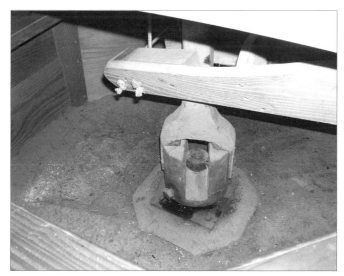

FIG 6.15: *An unusual view of an overdriven stone with the top runner stone removed. Moving from bottom up we see the neck box, the mace holding the drive shaft and lastly the shoe resting against the square shaft which acts as the damsel. This is Denver Mill.*

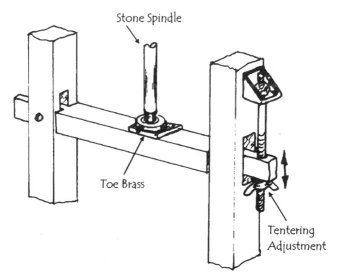

Stone Spindle

Toe Brass

Tentering Adjustment

FIG 6.16: *Basic tenter beam (or bridge tree). The beam which carries the stone drive shaft is pivoted at one end and the other end can be raised or lowered by means of a wing nut on a threaded shaft. This in turn raises or lowers the bearing, the shaft and the runner stone, so altering the gap between the two grinding stones. Note that the bottom bearing is in turn carried in a 'footstep bearing' and can be adjusted from side to side to get the shaft perfectly vertical.*

the spur wheel which itself was now near the ceiling rather than being below the floor.

We now come to a vital adjustment that was essential for the miller to be able to control – the gap between the stones. The adjustment was made by raising or lowering the bridge tree and thus the stone spindle and the runner stone itself. Called tentering, this adjustment was accomplished in several ways but all had in common the facility for the miller to adjust the gap whilst being able to see and feel the flour coming from the grind wheels. He would judge the coarseness and the temperature of the flour to decide if the gap needed to be altered. This was in fact quite a tricky job, the gap depending on many factors – the type of grain, the speed of the wheel, the quality of the flour needed and the rate at which the grain was being fed into the grindstones.

The other requirement was to be able to disengage the drive to the stone. This might be because only one pair of stones was required or it might be that the power was needed to operate the sack hoist or other machinery without any stones turning. Again a variety of mechanisms exist but all had the same task – to disconnect the stone nut from the spur wheel. With overdriven drive systems the entire drive shaft, complete with the stone nut, was usually moved over at the top thus disengaging the drive. With underdriven systems the shaft can't be moved – it carries the runner stone – so the stone nut slid up or down the shaft allowing it to be disengaged from the spur wheel.

As with the other gears it was standard practice to have wooden teeth on either

FIG 6.17: *A 'modern' tenter beam in cast iron from around the 1850s. Part of the Heckington Mill in Lincolnshire.*

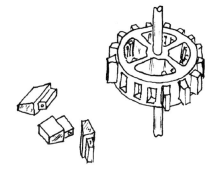

A. *Here the miller removes three or four cogs (called slip cogs) to leave a gap which is positioned opposite the spur wheel.*

C. *A close-up of the type of mechanism shown in Fig B. The block (called a glut box) with the retaining ring can be removed and the shaft then rests against the half bearing whilst working.*

FIG 6.18: *The way the stone nut is disengaged from the spur wheel makes an excellent example of the variations one finds. Here we look at three methods used for overdriven stones.*

B: *A more common method is to move the top of the drive shaft out of its bearing and hold it in an iron ring. This example is from Heckingtom Mill.*

D: *An alternative is to move the bearing itself aside. The bearing is carried on a beam which can be moved over. This example is in Brindley Mill.*

FIG 6.19: *With underdriven stones the shaft cannot be moved so the stone nut itself has to be moved out of mesh with the spur wheel.*

A. *This stone nut has a square hole through it which rides up and down over a square shaft. The wing nut below the stone nut winds it up and down. To be seen at Stretton Mill, in Cheshire.*

B: *This time a forked lever raises the stone nut out of mesh. It slides over a key-way which conveys the drive to the stone nut. This is Alderholt Mill in Hampshire.*

C: *A very common system where the stone nut is raised on a ring which is wound up from below (called a jack ring). The drive is via the square tapered shaft which runs through the stone nut. This example is from Bunbury Mill.*

the stone nut or the spur wheel to keep the noise level low.

Ancillary Drives

There could be a great number of grain cleaners and flour dressers in a mill, all needing power to drive them. This was sometimes taken from a 'crown' wheel and bevel gear that drove a shaft which in turn carried pulleys. The power was then taken via belts to the various machines, though provision had to be made to disengage the drive to each machine. This was usually achieved by a mechanism which allowed the belt to fall slack or to move it over onto a dummy pulley that simply ran free.

The Sack Hoist

This was another delightfully simple and effective device used to raise the sacks of grain or flour to the higher floors of the mill, originally done by the miller's assistant – often a young boy – carrying the sacks on his back as he climbed ladders from floor to floor (steps are a modern addition).

There are two key features: the friction clutch that allowed the drive to be activated by simply pulling on a rope, and the trap doors that allowed the sacks to rise through each floor but closed afterwards to prevent accidents and to allow the sacks to be put down. As always there are variations: some used a continuous chain, some a single chain or a single rope. In all cases, though, the winding drum (rather like the old fashioned winding gear used in a water well) was driven by pulling a rope which

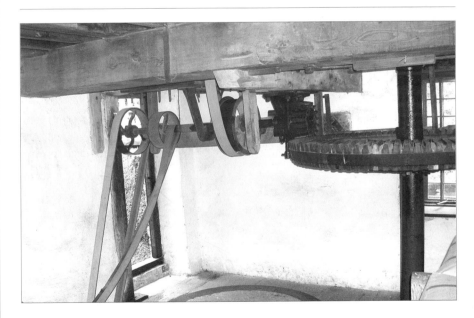

FIG 6.20: *Ancillary drive shaft driven from the crown wheel. In this photograph, from Dunster Mill in Somerset, the far pulley has the belt tight and is driving a cleaning machine whilst the nearest pulley, which drives the sack hoist, is slack.*

FIG 6.21: *Delightful re-creation of the miller controlling the sack hoist as a sack of grain arrives on the top floor of his mill. Brindley Mill, Staffordshire.*

passed down the mill close to the trap doors. Sometimes the control rope lifted a beam carrying the drive wheel so that it bore onto another wheel which was on the main drive shaft, sometimes it tightened a belt, allowing it to grip the pulleys and thus drive. Some drives had two control ropes, one engaging the drive, the other disconnecting it.

The sacks were attached to the chain or rope by twisting the top of the sack through a ring or loop. As the sack rose, it pushed the split trap doors open and once clear they simply crashed closed again. When the appropriate floor was reached the drive was released and the weight of the sack (often up to 2 cwt or 100 kg) slowly reversed the direction of the chain and the sack rested on the floor.

As I hope the last two chapters have shown, the mill really is a treasure trove of simple but ingenious mechanisms. Hopefully, the drawings and photos have made most features a little clearer!

FIG 6.22: *The sack hoist in Town Mill, Lyme Regis. The lever is raised by pulling the rope at the far end and in turn this tightens the belt to engage the drive. All the hoist mechanisms use some form of friction drive to prevent the rope being snatched or jerked as the drive is engaged.*

FIG 6.23:
Friction drive for the sack hoist in the Wilton windmill. By raising the winding axle the hoist drive wheel is pressed onto the under-side of a friction wheel and thus turns the winch

FIG 6.24: *Yet another sack hoist mechanism, this time from the Denver windmill in Norfolk. In this version the rope pulls a jockey wheel over to tighten the belt thus enabling the drive. As in most windmills this is right at the top of the tower.*

FIG 6.25: *Denver windmill in all its glory, a typical Norfolk mill with symmetrical sails and an ogee cap built in 1835. This mill also had an oil engine driving its own set of stones to cope with spells of no wind.*

CHAPTER 7

The Other Applications

We have looked at waterwheels used to grind corn to make flour but since Roman times the power from a waterwheel has been applied to other uses. The earliest was probably to lift water, either from a river for use in irrigation or out of mines. The Archimedes screw was used to raise water a few feet to irrigation channels, though this was often turned by animal or human effort. To lift over greater heights the 'chain of pots' idea was used. A variation on this was the 'rag and chain' pump in which a series of cloth bags were arranged around a continuous chain which was slowly turned by the

FIG 7.1: *Claverton pump, near Bath, is, by English standards, a large waterwheel which drives two water pumps. It was built in 1810 to lift 100,000 gallons of water each hour from the river Avon to the Kennet and Avon Canal some 14 m above.*

waterwheel. At the bottom the bags absorbed water which they held as they were raised. At the top they were drawn through a constricted pipe-way which squeezed the bags and thus wrung out the water – very inefficient since the power source had to both raise the water and then provide the energy needed to squeeze the bags. There are odd references to

these water-lifting machines throughout the medieval period but little that can be verified and indeed almost no applications are known here in Britain.

The first widespread non-milling use of water wheels in Britain was for fulling cloth. Documented in the 12th century, this may well have started earlier.

During the 12th to 16th centuries a

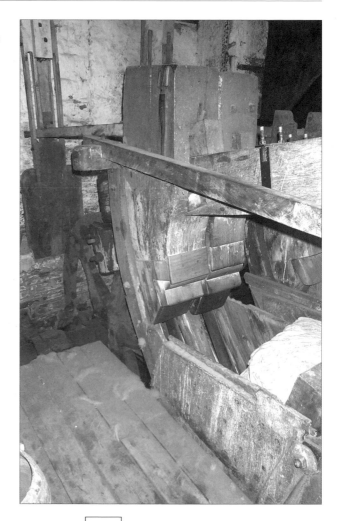

FIG 7.2: *Waterwheel-driven fulling stocks in the Helmshaw Mills Textile Museum, Lancashire. There are two hammers which alternate when in action. Here both are locked in the raised position to allow the cloth to be removed.*

FIG 7.3: *Cheddleton Mill in Staffordshire, like many water mills, had been used both for fulling and flour grinding in earlier times. Its final use was grinding flint for the china industry in nearby Stoke on Trent.*

FIG 7.4: *Inside Cheddleton Mill where the calcined flint was ground in water until it became a thick smooth slurry, a process that took around 24 hours. It was then dried and cut into slabs before transportation to Stoke on Trent for the pottery industries.*

great many other uses were made of the power provided by the waterwheel. It takes a few minutes' thought to imagine just how important these developments were. Prior to the waterwheel the only sources of power were animals and humans, both limited – each gets tired and both need feeding and looking after. Waterwheels provided a vast increase in the power without the limitations. There were three basic ways that this power was used: for rotary machines, for cam-driven hammers or bellows, and lastly, for crank-driven devices like pumps. I will not attempt to put the various uses into chronological order – there simply isn't enough evidence. Instead I'll look at each of the three mechanisms and the industries they served.

Firstly, the rotary machines use the basic rotation which comes naturally from the wheel. We have already seen its use to turn grindstones but this technique was also used in other areas. Malt was pulverised under rotating stones before being made into a mash for beer making, and some types of ore were also ground between rotating stones, including tin and gold.

An early variation on the flat grinding stone was the edge stone. Here the turning motion was used to move a round stone around a track on its edge. This was

FIG 7.5: *Trip hammer driven by a waterwheel at Wortley Forge, Yorkshire. No gearing was used, the wheel turned the trip wheel directly which in turn raised and dropped the hammer four times for each revolution.*

FIG 7.6: *An old horse-powered edge stone, used to crush rather than grind. This example is in the Avoncroft Museum of Historic Buildings. The slow steady rotation needed can easily be provided by a waterwheel.*

an old technique originally using a horse or donkey but dramatically improved by water power. Edge running stones were used to produce substances that needed a crushing action rather than the cutting and grinding action of rotary stones. Olive oil, poppy seed, mustard seed and sugar cane were all treated this way, as were sources of dyes and pigments – produced by crushing bark and wood. Tannin was made by first crushing oak bark from which the tannin was then leached out. The other important use was to crush minerals – mortar, snuff, pipe clay and even gunpowder were all made this way. Mineral slurries for the china

industry were produced by crushing pre-heated flint stone – a use that survived into the 20th century.

Another use of rotating stones was polishing and grinding, extensively employed in the Sheffield area for cutlery, swords and industrial cutting blades.

The last processes that used the basic rotating power were what today we would think of as machines – boring machines and iron rolling mills. These were the first industrial tools, in use long before the Industrial Revolution. Boring machines were used first to bore out wooden water pipes and then to bore true and smooth holes in iron – for

FIG 7.7: *In its day (15th–17th centuries) the most important use of a waterwheel after making flour was driving bellows for ironmaking. This drawing shows the principle of the most common arrangement. The waterwheel pushes the bellows closed and the weighted boxes pull the bellows open again.*

cannons and later engine and pump cylinders.

Waterwheel-driven slitting mills arrived as early as the 1500s. Iron that had been hammered into crude flat strips was reheated and passed through a revolving cutter that gave the strip straight even edges – ideal for wagon wheel tyres and barrel bands. Iron was also shaped by passing the red hot wrought iron through rollers that progressively flattened it into strips, rods and bars.

By the 17th century, small workshops equipped with lathes and numerous other machines were relatively common – all using waterwheels to provide the power.

The second group of machines used cams, usually to provide some form of impact. The basic principle of the cam is that the rotating motion from the waterwheel lifts a heavy hammer and then lets it drop free under its own weight. A great many applications were made of this action, including fulling woollen cloth, pounding rags for papermaking, crushing ore and stone. One vitally important sector of our embryo industrial scene was ironmaking and this needed bellows to produce an air blast to keep the furnaces hot. Waterwheel-driven bellows were used throughout all the early ironmaking areas

FIG 7.8: *The use of cams but not to raise and drop hammers. Here the two beautifully curved cams, driven by a waterwheel just outside the building, operate the two air pumps at the top of the picture.*
These supplied air to a coke fired hearth, a 'modern' version of Fig 7.7. This is in the Abbeydale Scythe works, near Sheffield.

and indeed were still employed in forging iron right into the 20th century. Once the malleable wrought iron was hot enough it could be beaten into shape. Originally done by hand-held hammers, this work lent itself to water-driven hammers, particularly when the object being forged was large.

The last group of machines used a crank turned by the rotating action of the wheel. Whilst more difficult to make than a cam – most crank applications had to wait until ironwork was firmly established – cranks provided a true push and pull action. This was ideal for sawing and pumping and indeed these two

FIG 7.9: *Inside the wheel shed of the Claverton pump (see Fig 7.1). One of the largest wheels (18 ft diameter by 25 ft wide) that is still regularly demonstrated, this drove two pumps via a system of cranks.*

FIG 7.10: *A 1902 pitchback wheel which drives a triple water pump by means of cranks. Originally used in Dorset to pump water from the river Frome to the Duke of Somerset's estate, it is now on display in the Kew Bridge Steam museum in London.*

FIG 7.11: *Another unusual application, this time in Cornwall. This 18 ft (5.5 m) diameter overshot wheel drove china clay slurry pumps by means of a crank and a series of rods that carried the to and fro motion from the wheel to the pumps in the clay pit. Part of the Wheal Martyn China Clay Museum.*

FIG 7.12: *An example of machinery that was driven by a waterwheel. This is Whitchurch Silk Mill where the waterwheel (in the wooden extension at the right and still turning) was originally used to operate silk spinning and winding machines.*

applications accounted for the vast majority of crank systems. Most large estates had a small sawing mill for their own needs and some timber supply companies had large mills with upward of 40 saws in use driven from one large waterwheel. The circular saw was invented in 1777 and lent itself to the original rotation produced by the waterwheel.

Some of the mining areas made vast use of water power. Possibly the largest was in Devon where in the 1840s a stream with a drop of some 500 ft (150 m) powered 17 wheels, one after the other, the last wheel being 50 ft (15 m) in diameter and 10 ft (3 m) in width. Eight of the wheels were used for pumping, four for raising ore from the mines and the other five for crushing the ores.

There were also many other specialist uses that I've not mentioned but like so many of the artefacts from before the 19th century, very little is left for us to see today other than examples from the main large scale applications.

I have mentioned the small workshop which would have used a waterwheel to power its machines, a concept which was taken up by the vast textile factories of the late 1700s. Here quite awe-inspiring wheels would power an entire three or four storey factory, driving hundreds of machines – alas, they were usually ousted by steam engines in the 1800s and very little remains to be seen. One of the largest ever built in Britain was for Shaw's cotton spinning works in Greenock, Scotland. This was a pitchback wheel 70 ft (20 m) tall and 13 ft (3.8 m) wide which developed some 200 hp.

Looking at the examples we have left it is easy to assume that the windmill was rather left out of this diverse application of early power. But in fact they were applied to driving grinding, beating and even sawing machines, though their main use apart from flour grinding was pumping water for drainage as pioneered by the Dutch. They could never produce the ever-expanding power levels demanded by industry and this plus the unreliability of the wind probably explains the early demise of these alternative uses. Whilst flour and animal feed grinding could wait for days if need be, most industrial processes couldn't. Even though streams can run dry in a hot summer this is an event that can be predicted, possibly weeks in advance, unlike the wind which may vanish with but an hour's notice.

Section III

Restored Mills

to

Visit

CHAPTER 8

The Scene Today

＊＋ ⌁◈⌁ ＋＊

As I have already hinted at in the last chapter, mills either lingered on or they vanished. The fact that so much of the early mills' construction was wooden meant that, once abandoned, the building soon collapsed and rejoined nature.

Today, though, we still have a good selection of both waterwheels and windmills which were either built or, at least, very extensively refurbished, in the 1800s. Sufficient structure survived for the gallant bands of restorers to rebuild and repair. Many mills are a mixture of machines from other less fortunate sites, but all are lovingly tended by enthusiastic owners or trusts.

Ironically the restoration is usually of such a high standard that to most visitors the mills look as we imagine they were

FIG 8.1: *Town Mill in Lyme Regis, not quite what one expects at the seaside. This mill is in fact very old and beautifully restored with excellent guides.*

hundreds of years ago. The story of the struggles that the restorers go through could almost fill a book on its own but I will summarise a typical story taken from the handbook for the Greens windmill in Nottingham:

Having fallen into disuse around 1868 the sails were removed for safety reasons and the mill left to slowly rot. Sometime after 1900 the huge oak fantail frame fell from the back of the cap and crashed through the roof of the foreman's cottage, destroying – it is said – a grand piano. The damage was so severe that the cottage was demolished. Used as a dovecote for a while, the mill then changed hands until in 1923 the cap was covered in copper to keep the rain out. It was then let to a firm of furniture polish makers until 1947 when a fire wreaked havoc. Everything bar a few stout floor beams had gone including the cap. The owner had a concrete slab built over the top to keep the weather at bay and the mill was left for 30 more years – a very sad and neglected sight. It was the fact that the original miller, George Green, had been a brilliant mathematician that created enough interest to prevent the mill being demolished. In 1979 the mill was handed over to the council who after many more false starts realised the enormous educational and tourism potential of the project and decided that it should be part of the city's museum service. Plans were drawn up to replace the mill yard buildings (which had fallen into complete ruin and had been cleared away) with new buildings in a style and in materials sympathetic to the 175-year-old windmill. In 1984 a derelict cottage adjacent to the site was restored as accommodation for the newly-appointed Mill Custodian. The project picked up momentum again as the restoration was now in the hands of professional millwrights, R Thompson and Son of Alford. Getting the mill into full working order was to be a much longer process than had been anticipated and many problems were encountered. But, on 2nd December 1986 the millwrights spread the canvas cloths upon the common sails, closed the shutters of the spring sails and released the brake. The sails turned and for the first time since the 1860s flour was produced at Greens Mill.

This brief story leaves out the endless problems that had to be overcome, not least of getting the building through the barren 1960–1980 period and into the new dawn of restoration. It is quite remarkable just how many windmills and waterwheels came through this sort of struggle to be with us today.

Windmills tend to be by far the most visually obvious structures due to their basic need to be exposed to the winds. Waterwheels on the other hand are often hidden in the bottom of small valleys where streams still run carelessly ever downwards. Many watermills had the waterwheel contained within the building adding to the darkness and, alas, the difficulty of getting good photographs.

There are still a great many reminders of milling history all around us. Most towns and many villages still have a 'Mill Lane'. Some sites are commemorated with information boards even though very little of the mill remains to be seen.

There are several approaches to locating mills in one's own area. Often local libraries, museums or tourist offices will have information. You can also search on the web but you will need to keep the criteria local or you will be drowned in unhelpful data.

Looking at Ordnance Survey maps can be useful – just follow the small rivers

FIG 8.2: *One I did manage to capture – the overshot wheel that drives the Town Mill in Lyme Regis. The leat which has travelled some quarter of a mile to gain height, turns through the wall of the mill and under the sluice gate.*

FIG 8.3: *The leat en route – the leat is to the left of the footpath, whilst the river tumbles ever downwards towards the sea.*

FIG 8.4: *A timely reminder of what happens if a restored mill is not cared for. This windmill in Dereham, Cambridgeshire, is showing the first signs of serious problems – look at the sails!*

FIG 8.5: *Another mill in the care of the National Trust, Lode Watermill on the Anglesea Abbey estate in Cambridgeshire. The waterwheel can just be seen in the bottom left corner of the building. Built in the 18th century, it was used at the end of its working life to produce cement but is fortunately now restored and producing flour once again.*

and streams, in particular looking for small lakes which are likely to be old mill ponds. Remember, though, that the word 'mill' probably signifies a private house or building that was once a mill. Following higher ground will often reveal a windmill sign and in Lincolnshire, Norfolk, Suffolk and Kent there are many windmills shown on tourist maps, though not all are necessarily open or working.

Today's working mills tend to fall into three groups. Those that are maintained by large trusts like English Heritage or the National Trust, or are lucky enough to have a large band of helpers, are open throughout the summer months and often in the winter months as well. The second group, typically run by volunteers from local trusts or societies, open regularly at weekends, but usually only in the summer months. The last group tend to be mills that are in private ownership where the

FIG 8.6: *I have used many close-up pictures to explain specific mechanisms but here are a few pictures to give an idea of what you see inside a working mill. This is just one part of the Longbridge Mill, in Hampshire, showing the full set of four stones.*

owners have restored the machinery, and are open to the public on specific days only.

Finally, the Mills Section of the Society for the Preservation of Historic Buildings publishes a book called *Mills Open* which lists over 400 sites open to the public.

A further excellent source of information is the series of regional leaflets produced by local mills groups. Published annually, these usually contain the latest information and opening times.

Listed below is a selection of sites which are open at least one day per week during the summer (May to September). Beware, though, many only open in the afternoon. Some sites have complicated rotas and may be open more often than shown, particularly in school holidays. Always phone if making a long journey as most rely on volunteers and times can change at short notice. What you can see also varies. Some sites have non-working machinery on view through glass panels. Others have full working machines, produce flour for sale and have superb guides.

Do remember that many sites have working machinery, steep stairways and low beams and ceilings, so please keep children under control, mind your head, and definitely no smoking!

FIG 8.7: *Another watermill – Daniels Mill in Shropshire where the owners take visitors around.*

FIG 8.8: *Dunster Mill in Somerset, leased from the National Trust, and thought to date from the late 1600s. This winnowing machine still cleans the flour before it is bagged and it's still driven from the waterwheel.*

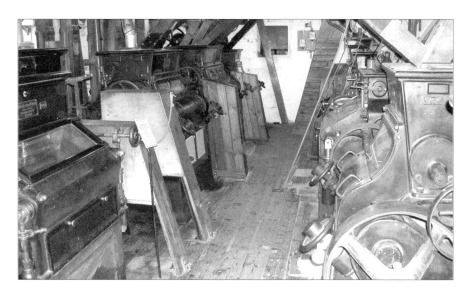

FIG 8.9: *A possibly unique sight, a set of early German-built roller mills. This is just one part of the displays at the Cauldwell Mill, in Derbyshire.*

FIG 8.10: *This is Nether Auderley Mill in Cheshire, owned by the National Trust and watched over by a band of dedicated enthusiasts. The building dates from the 15th century and has a fascinating history.*

Sites to Visit

Websites to try:
English Heritage   www.english-heritage.org.uk
The National Trust   www.nationaltrust.org.uk
Society for the Protection of Ancient Buildings   www.spab.org.uk/mills/

This is just a selection from the many mills that open. All opening times are taken from the latest *Mills Open* book but they do change – always try and phone before setting out unless you have an up-to-date leaflet. Many windmills can be seen even when not open but please respect private land and property.

Mills that feature an industrial application as opposed to milling are marked *

Bedford
Barton Water Wheel, Barton-le-Clay. 3 miles N of Luton. Part of Garden Centre.
Telephone: 01582 882929.

Bromham Watermill. 1 mile W of Bedford. (Sun & BH)
Telephone: 01234 824330.

Buckinghamshire
Lacey Green Windmill. 2 miles SE of Princes Risborough. (Sun & BH)
Telephone: 01844 343560.

Cambridgeshire
Houghton Watermill. 3 miles SE of Huntingdon. (Sat, Sun & BH) NT.
Telephone: 01480 301494.

Lode Watermill, Anglesey Abbey. 6 miles NE of Cambridge. (Wed to Sun & BH) NT.
Telephone: 01223 811260.

Sacrewell Watermill, Thornhaugh. 8 miles W of Peterborough. (Daily)
Telephone: 01780 782254.

*Wicken Fen Pumping Mill, Wicken Fen Nature Reserve. 9 miles SE of Ely (Daily) NT.
Telephone: 01353 720274.

Houghton Mill

Cheshire
Bunbury Watermill. (Sun & BH)
Telephone: 01829 261422.

*Dunham Massey Sawmill. 3 miles SW
of Altrincham. (Sat to Weds, pm) NT.
Telephone: 0161 928 4351.

Nether Alderley Watermill. 1½ miles S of
Alderley Edge.
(Wed to Fri, plus Sun & BH) NT.
Telephone: 01625 584412.

Stretton Watermill, nr Farndon. 10 miles S of
Chester. (Tue to Sun & BH)
Telephone: 01606 41331.

Bunbury Mill

Cleveland
Tocketts Watermill. 1½ miles NE of
Guisborough. (Sun)

Cornwall
*Wheal Martyn Waterwheel Pumps,
Carthew. 2 miles NW of St Austell.
Part of China Clay Museum. (Daily)
Telephone: 01726 850362.

Stretton Mill

Melinsey Watermill, Veryan, Truro. (Daily except Mon)
Telephone: 01872 501371.

Trewey Watermill, Zennor. 4½ miles W of St Ives. (Daily)
Part of Wayside Folk Museum.
Telephone: 01736 796945.

Cumbria
Heron Corn Mill, Beetham. 6 miles N of Carnforth. (Tue to Sun & BH)
Telephone: 01539 565027.

Gleaston Mill, nr Ulverston. Signs from Aldingham. (Tue to Sun & BH)
Telephone: 01229 869244.

Little Salkeld Mill, nr Penrith. 1½ miles NE of Langwathby. (Daily, not Sat)
Telephone: 01768 881523.

Derbyshire

Caudwell Mill, Rowsley. Unusual mill using turbines and early roller mills. (Daily)
Telephone: 01629 734374.

Heage Windmill. Superb six-sail windmill. 2 miles NE of Belper. (Sat, Sun & BH)
Telephone: 01773 853579.

Stainsby Mill, Hardwick Hall. 7 miles W of Mansfield. (Wed, Thur, Sat, Sun & BH) NT.
Telephone: 01246 850430.

Devon

Bicclescombe Waterwheel, Ilfracombe. (Daily)
Telephone: 01271 862834.

Bickleigh Watermill. 4 miles S of Tiverton. (Daily)
Telephone: 01884 855419.

Heage Mill

Hele Mill, Ilfracombe. 1 mile E of Ilfracombe. (Daily but not Sun in June or Sept)
Telephone: 01271 863185.

*Morwellham. 1 mile SE of Gunnislake. Site has four waterwheels including underground mine drainage wheel. (Daily)
Telephone: 01822 833808.

Otterton Watermill, nr Budleigh Salterton. (Daily)
Telephone: 01395 568521.

*Finch Foundry, Sticklepath. 4 miles E of Okehampton. (Daily except Tues) NT.
Telephone: 0187 840046.

Dorset

Place Watermill, Christchurch Quay. (Daily)
Telephone: 01202 487626.

Town Mill, Lyme Regis.
(Tue to Sun plus BH)
Telephone: 01297 443579.

Mangerton Watermill, nr Powerstock. 4
miles NE of Bridport. (Tue to Sun plus
BH) Telephone: 01308 485224.

White Mill, Shapwick. 7 miles SE of
Blandford Forum. (Sat, Sun & BH) NT
Telephone: 01258 857184

Town Mill

Sturminster Newton Watermill (turbine not
wheel). 9 miles NW of Blandford Forum. (Thur, Sat, Sun & BH Mon)
Telephone: 01747 854355.

County Durham
*Killhope Lead Mining Centre (waterwheels). On A689, 8 miles SE of Alston. (Daily)
Telephone: 01388 537505.

Essex
Bourne Watermill. S of Colchester off B1025. (Tue & Sun) NT.
Telephone: 01206 572422.

John Webb's Windmill, Thaxted. 10 miles NE of Bishop's Stortford. (Sat, Sun & BH)
Telephone: 01371 830285.

Greater London
House Mill, Three Mills, Bromley By Bow. Tidal mill. (Sun afternoons)
Telephone: 020 8539 6726.

Merton Abbey Mills. Off A24 nr Superstore. (Sat, Sun & BH)
Telephone: 020 8543 9608.

Wimbledon Windmill. On Wimbledon
Common. Signed from A219. (Sat, Sun & BH)
Telephone: 020 8947 2825.

Hampshire
Alderholt Mill. 2 miles SW of Fordingbridge.
(Sat, Sun & BH)
Telephone: 01425 653130.

Alderholt Mill

Bursledon Windmill. Signed from Jn 8 of M27. (Sat & Sun)
Telephone: 02380 404999.

Eling Tide Mill. 3 miles W of Southampton. (Wed to Sun & BH)
Telephone: 0238 0869575.

Longbridge Watermill, Sherfield on Loddon. 5 miles NE of Basingstoke. (Daily)
Telephone: 01256 883483.

City Mill, Winchester. E side of city centre. (Wed to Sun)
Telephone: 01962 870057.

Bursledon Mill

Hertfordshire
Cromer Windmill, Ardeley. 6 miles NE of Stevenage. (Sun & BH)
Telephone: 01438 861662.

Mill Green Watermill, Hatfield. Signed from Jn 4 of A1(M). (Tue to Sun & BH)
Telephone: 01707 271362.

Kingsbury Watermill, St Albans. 2 miles SE of St Albans. (Daily)
Telephone: 01727 853502.

Isle of Wight
Bembridge Windmill. S of Bembridge. (Daily except Sat) NT.
Telephone: 01983 884167.

Calbourne Watermill. 1 mile W of Calbourne. (Daily)
Telephone: 01983 531227.

Kent
Union Windmill, Cranbrook. (Sat & BH)
Telephone: 01580 712984.

Crabble Watermill, Dover. 2 miles NW of Dover, nr River. (Daily)
Telephone: 01304 823292.

Bembridge Mill

*Chart Gunpowder Mills, Faversham. (Sat, Sun & BH)
Telephone: 01795 534542.

Meopham Windmill, Meopham Green. 6 miles S of Gravesend. (Sun & BH)
Telephone: 01474 813518.

Sarre Windmill. 10 miles W of Ramsgate. (Tue to Sun)
Telephone: 01843 847573.

Woodchurch Windmill. 7 miles SW of Ashford. (Sun & BH)
Telephone: 01233 860649.

Lancashire
Marsh Windmill, Thornton Cleveleys. 4 miles N of Blackpool. (Daily)
Telephone: 01253 860765.

Lincolnshire
Alford Windmill. 8 miles SW of Mablethorpe. (Daily)
Telephone: 01507 462136.

Maud Foster Windmill, Boston.
(Wed, Sat & Sun)
Telephone: 01205 352188.

Heckington Windmill. 12 miles W of Boston. (Thu
to Sun & BH)
Telephone: 01529 461919.

Hewitt's Windmill, Heapham. 5 miles SE of
Gainsborough. (Sat & BH)
Telephone: 01427 838230.

Ellis's Windmill, Lincoln. Nr Cathedral. (Sat & Sun)
Telephone: 01522 528448.

Trader Windmill, Sibsey. 5 miles N of Boston. (Tue,
Sat, Sun & BH)
Telephone: 01205 750036.

Maud Foster Mill

Cogglesford Watermill, Sleaford. NE of town. (Daily)
Telephone: 01529 414294.

Waltham Windmill, 4 miles S of Grimsby. (Sat, Sun & BH)
Telephone: 01472 822236.

Norfolk
Cley Windmill, Cley next the Sea. 12 miles W of Sheringham. (Daily PM)
Telephone: 01263 740209.

Denver Windmill. 2 miles S of Downham
Market. (Daily)
Telephone: 01366 384009.

Great Bircham Windmill. 12 miles NE of
Kings Lynn. (Daily)
Telephone: 01485 578393.

Letheringsett Watermill. 1 mile W of
Holt. (Daily except Sun)
Telephone: 01263 713153.

Sutton Windmill. 15 miles NW of Gt
Yarmouth, E of village. (Daily)
Telephone: 01692 581195.

*Thurne Dyke Drainage Mill.
10 miles NW of Gt Yarmouth.
(Most Suns – phone)
Telephone: 01603 222705.

Denver Mill

Northumbria
Heatherslaw Watermill, Etal. 10 miles
SW of Berwick-upon-Tweed. (Daily)
Telephone: 01890 820338.

Otterburn Mill. 25 miles NW of
Newcastle. (Daily)
Telephone: 01830 520225.

Nottinghamshire
North Leverton Windmill. 5 miles E of
Retford. (Most Sun PM)
Telephone: 01427 880573.

Greens Windmill, Sneinton. 1 mile E of
Nottingham centre. (Wed to Sun & BH)
Telephone: 0115 915 6878.

Greens Mill

Ollerton Watermill. Nr town centre. (Sun & BH)
Telephone: 01623 822469.

Oxfordshire
Chinnor Windmill. NW edge of Chinnor village. (Occasional Suns, but outside at any time.) Telephone: 01844 292095.

Mapledurham Watermill. 3 miles NW of Reading. Approach from A4074.
(Sat, Sun & BH)
Telephone: 0118 947 8284.

Shropshire
Daniels Watermill, Bridgnorth. ½ mile S
on B4555. (Wed, Sat, Sun & BH)
Telephone: 01746 762753.

Somerset & Bristol
Ashton Windmill, Chapel Allerton. 8
miles SE of Weston-super-Mare. (Sun &
BH) Telephone: 01934 712034.

Bishops Lydeard Watermill. 6 miles NW
of Taunton. (Tue to Fri, Sun & BH)
Telephone: 01823 432151.

Daniels Mill

Burcott Watermill, 2 miles W of Wells on
B3139. (Daily except Mon)
Telephone: 01749 673118.

*Claverton Pumping Station. 3 miles E of
Bath, Ferry Lane. (Sun, Wed & BH)
Telephone: 0117 986 5264.

Dunster Watermill. 2 miles SE of
Minehead. (Daily except Fri) NT.
Telephone: 01643 821759.

Stembridge Windmill, High Ham. 9 miles SE
of Bridgwater. (Sun, Mon, Wed)
Telephone: 01458 25081.

Burcott Mill

*Wookey Hole Paper Mill. 2 miles NW of Wells. (Daily)
Telephone: 01749 672243.

Staffordshire
Brindley Watermill, Leek. ½ mile NW from town centre. (Sat, Sun & BH)
Telephone: 01538 360900.

*Cheddleton Flint Mill. 2 miles S of
Leek, adjacent to canal. (Sat to Wed)
Telephone: 01782 502907.

Shugborough Estate Watermill. 6 miles E
of Stafford. (Daily except Mon) NT.
Telephone: 01889 881388.

Suffolk
Pakenham Watermill, Ixworth. 7 miles
NE of Bury St Edmunds.
(Wed, Sat, Sun & BH)
Telephone: 01359 270570.

Cheddleton Mill

Pakenham Windmill, Ixworth. Approx.
½ mile S of village. (Daily)
Telephone: 01359 230277.

Saxtead Green Windmill. 26 miles E of
Bury St Edmunds. (Mon to Sat) EH.
Telephone: 01728 685789.

Museum of East Anglian Life, Stowmarket.
Includes wind pump and watermill. (Daily)
Telephone: 01449 612229.

Pakenham Mill

Buttrum's Windmill, Woodbridge. ½ mile W
of town centre. (Sat, Sun & BH)
Telephone: 01473 583352.

Woodbridge Tide Mill. On quayside. (Daily)
Telephone: 01473 626618.

Surrey
Painshill Park Waterwheel, Cobham. Off A245. (Tue to Sun & BH)
Telephone: 01932 868113.

Haxted Watermill Museum, 2 miles W of Edenbridge. (Daily except Mon)
Telephone: 01732 862914.

Outwood Windmill. 6 miles SE of Redhill, ½ mile E of village. (Sun)
Telephone: 01342 843458.

Sussex
Jill Windmill, Clayton. 7 miles N of
Brighton. (Sun)
Telephone: 01273 843263.

Polegate Windmill. 4 miles N of
Eastbourne. (Sun & BH)
Telephone: 01323 644727.

Stone Cross Windmill. 3 miles N of
Eastbourne. (Sun)
Telephone: 01323 763206.

West Blatchington Windmill, 1 mile N of
Hove. (Sun)
Telephone: 01273 776017.

Shipley Windmill, nr Horsham. 5 miles
SE of Billingshurst. (Most Sun & BH)
Telephone: 01403 730439.

Jill Mill

Weald and Downland Museum, Singleton. Waterwheel & windpump.
7 miles N of Chichester. (Daily)
Telephone: 01243 811363.

Tyne and Wear
Pathhead Watermill, Blaydon. 2 miles SW of Newcastle. (Daily)
Telephone: 0191 414 6288.

Fulwell Windmill. On A1018, 2 miles N of Sunderland. (Sun)
Telephone: 0191 516 9790.

Warwickshire
Chesterton Windmill. 7 miles SE of Warwick. Unique structure,
only visible from outside.
Telephone: 01926 412033.

Wellesbourne Watermill. ½ mile S of Wellesbourne. (Thu to Sun)
Telephone: 01789 470237.

Wiltshire
Wilton Windmill. 8 miles SE of
Marlborough, E of Wilton village.
(Sun & BH)
Telephone: 01672 870202.

Worcestershire
Avoncroft Museum. 2 miles S of
Bromsgrove.
Buildings museum with excellent post
mill. (Tue to Sun)
Telephone: 01527 831363.

Wilton Mill

Yorkshire
Skidby Windmill. 7 miles NW of Hull.
(Wed to Sun & BH)
Telephone: 01482 392773.

*Elvington Brickyard Windpump. 8 miles SE of York. (Daily)
Telephone: 01904 608 2255.

Fountains Abbey Watermill. Part of Fountains Abbey, 4 miles W of Ripon.
(Daily) NT.
Telephone: 01765 608888.

*Abbeydale Industrial Hamlet. 4 miles SW of
Sheffield. Superb industrial application of
waterwheels. (Mon to Thu and Sun)
Telephone: 0114 236 7731.

Bedgreave New Mill, Rother Valley Park. 8 miles E
of Sheffield, off A618. (Daily)
Telephone: 0114 247 1452.

Worsborough Watermill. 3 miles S of Barnsley.
(Wed to Sun & BH)
Telephone: 01226 774527.

*Top Forge, Wortley. 5 miles SW of Barnsley. (Sun
& BH)
Telephone: 0114 288 7576.

*Thwaite Mills, Leeds. (Sat & Sun)
Telephone: 0113 249 6453.

Top Forge

Stretton Watermill in Cheshire. A delightful example of the changes that were made to mills over the years. The timber and sandstone building houses two wheels, one from around 1770, the other from 1850. Inside is a wonderful mixture of old timbers and working grindstones.

BALCONY	See Reefing Gallery
BED STONE	The lower, stationary mill stone.
BOLTER	A dressing machine using a loose cloth sieve.
BRAKE WHEEL	Large gearwheel on the windshaft in windmills.
BREASTSHOT WHEEL	The water source reaches the wheel level with the shaft.
BRIDGE TREE	Beam that carries the stone shaft.
BURR STONE	The hardest mill stone material, found near Paris.
CANISTER	Cast-iron fixture that holds the two main sail stocks.
CAP	The protective structure at the top of a windmill.
COGS	The teeth of gear wheels used in mills, often wooden.
COMMON SAIL	Open frame sail over which a cloth sail is set.
CROWN WHEEL	A gear with the teeth facing upwards like a crown.
CURB	The top edge of a windmill tower on which the cap turns which bears the weight of the cap and sail.
DAMSEL	Shaped shaft which vibrates the shoe.
DRESSER	See Flour Dresser.
DRESSING	Cutting grooves in a grindstone's surface to break grain down faster.
FANTAIL	Small wind-powered fan used to steer the main sails into the wind.
FLOATS	The paddles on a waterwheel.
FLOUR DRESSER	Machine for grading the milled flour.
GLUT BOX	An adjustable bearing housing.
GOVERNOR	A device to adjust the tentering in response to speed.
GRITSTONE	Hard stone usually from the Derbyshire Peaks.
GUDGEON	Iron pin used to strengthen wheel shaft.
HOPPER	Container set above the grindstones to hold the grain.
HORSE	A four-legged stand that supports the shoe and hopper.
JACK RING	Ring used to lift the stone nut out of gear.
LEAT	Channel to carry water to a waterwheel.
MACE	A casting connecting the rhynd to the damsel or quant.
MEAL	Freshly ground grain, before any dressing.
MILL BILL	Chisel used to dress the stones.
NECKBOX	Bearing in the centre of the bed stone through which the stone spindle passes.
OGEE CAP	Onion-shaped cap on a windmill.
OVERDRIVEN	The runner stone is driven from above (typically windmill).
OVERSHOT WHEEL	The water source reaches the wheel level with its top.
PATENT SAIL	A shuttered sail that can be controlled whilst the sail is turning.
PITCHBACK WHEEL	An overshot wheel where the water source is reversed in direction, i.e. so the wheel now turns in the same direction as a breastshot wheel would have done.
PIT WHEEL	The large gear wheel on the wheel shaft in a waterwheel.
POLL END	The end of a windshaft, shaped so that sail stocks can be fixed through it.

POST MILL	An early windmill that turns around on a stout post.
QUANT	A shaft in an overdriven mill which takes power from the stone nut to the mace and stones.
QUERN	Basic grindstone powered by hand.
REEFING GALLERY	Walkway constructed around the mill to give access to the sails and control chains.
RHYND	A metal bar across the eye of the runner stone to support it on the vertical spindle.
ROLLER MILL	Modern mill using rollers to break down the grain.
RUNNER STONE	The top stone of a pair which turns.
SACK HOIST	A hoist used to lift sacks of grain or flour upwards in a mill.
SAIL CROSS	Cast-iron cross which carries the sails on a windmill.
SHADES	The individual shutters on a spring or patent sail.
SHOE	The guide down which the grain is shaken before dropping into the stones for grinding.
SLIP COG	The system of removing a number of teeth from the stone nut to disengage the drive.
SMOCK MILL	A form of tower mill built from a wooden frame.
SPOUT	The wooden tubes down which grain and flour flow.
SPRING SAIL	A basic sail using shutters controlled by a spring which can only be adjusted when stationary.
SPUR WHEEL	The largest gear in a mill which drives the stone nuts.
STEEL YARD	A steel arm running between the governor and the tenter beam.
STOCKS	The main arms that carry the sails in a windmill.
STONE NUT	Small gear that drives the runner stone via a quant or spindle.
STRIKING ROD	Long rod that passes through the sail shaft to operate patent shutters.
TAIL-WIND	To have a windmill positioned with the wind blowing from behind the sails.
TAILPOLE	Stout pole used to turn a windmill around.
TENTER BEAM	Beam that carries the runner stone and controls the gap between the stones.
TENTERING	Mechanism for controlling the gap between the stones.
TOWER MILL	Stone- or brick-built windmill.
TUN	Container built around the grinding stones to keep the flour in.
UNDERDRIVEN	The runner stone is driven from below (typically waterwheel).
UNDERSHOT WHEEL	The water source flows under the wheel.
VAT	See Tun
WALLOWER	The gear that drives the main vertical shaft in the mill.
WIND ENGINE	Windmill that simply provides rotating power for other external machines to use.
WINDSHAFT	The main shaft that carries the sails in a windmill.
WIRE MACHINE	Sieving or dressing machine that uses a rotary wire sieve.

ALSO IN THIS SERIES

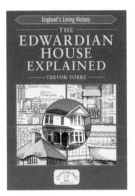

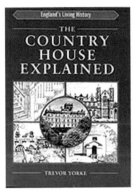

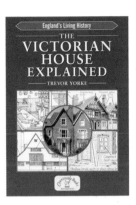

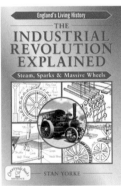

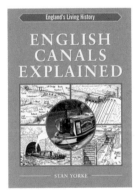

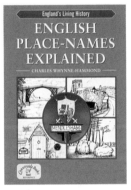

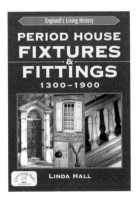

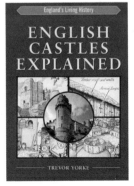

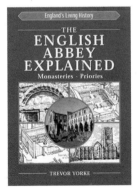